THE AMERICAN EPIDEMIC

"I was almost despondent to believe that the kids under the age of one, babies under age one, were receiving this kind of medication."

—United States Senator Thomas Carper,
lead requestor of the 2011 GAO Child Foster Care report,
and Chairman of the Homeland Security
and Government Affairs Committee.

"Eye-Opening. A change in our attitudes, thinking and our actions is called for. Granett has taken a bold step in helping parents, teachers, politicians and medical professionals educate themselves to help our children."

—Don Rush, columnist and assistant publisher,
The Clarkston News.

"They subverted science and induced others to betray people they were supposed to be taking care of. To me that is reprehensible."

—Allen Jones, former investigator of Pennsylvania's Office of
Inspector General, Bureau of Special Investigations,
and plaintiff vs. Johnson & Johnson.

"The American Epidemic: Solutions for Over-medicating Our Youth is an informative read, advocating a positive action plan for the American educational system in children with behavioral conditions."

—Bart Clark, Independence Township Superintendent

theAmerican
EPIDEMIC

Solutions for

OVER-MEDICATING

Our Youth

Frank J. Granett R.ph.

NEW YORK

the American EPIDEMIC
Solutions for OVER-MEDICATING *Our Youth*

Published in New York, New York, by Morgan James Publishing. Morgan James and The Entrepreneurial Publisher are trademarks of Morgan James, LLC. www.MorganJamesPublishing.com

The Morgan James Speakers Group can bring authors to your live event. For more information or to book an event visit The Morgan James Speakers Group at www.TheMorganJamesSpeakersGroup.com.

FREE eBook edition for your existing eReader with purchase

PRINT NAME ABOVE

For more information, instructions, restrictions, and to register your copy, go to **www.bitlit.ca/readers/register** or use your QR Reader to scan the barcode:

ISBN 978-1-63047-052-4 paperback
ISBN 978-1-63047-053-1 eBook
ISBN 978-1-63047-051-7 hardcover
Library of Congress Control Number: 2014931466

Cover Design by:
Rachel Lopez
www.r2cdesign.com

Interior Design by:
Bonnie Bushman
bonnie@caboodlegraphics.com

In an effort to support local communities, raise awareness and funds, Morgan James Publishing donates a percentage of all book sales for the life of each book to Habitat for Humanity Peninsula and Greater Williamsburg.

Get involved today, visit
www.MorganJamesBuilds.com

Habitat for Humanity
Peninsula and Greater Williamsburg Building Partner

Contents

Introduction

Medications used to treat attention deficit hyperactivity disorder (ADHD), autism spectrum disorder (ASD) as well as psychiatric disorders are being prescribed to children and young adults at an alarming epidemic rate. Over 12 million children and young adults consume ADHD stimulant and psychiatric medications. This rate of consumption represents 3x the world's children combined, according to data collected by *Scientific American.* More alarmingly, this statistic will jeopardize the health and well- being of our next generation if not immediately addressed.

The American Epidemic offers constructive guidance to parents, educators, healthcare professionals, policymakers, and the drug industry for the purpose of realizing the dangers of overmedicating our youth. Advertising these drugs via television and radio broadcasts by the pharmaceutical industry, devoid of complete educational information, is fueling the demand.

The ADHD and ASD epidemic has caused the Behavioral Health Crisis in America due to premature use of powerful stimulant and psychiatric medications in young children prior to ruling out nutritional, physiological, or environmental causes to their behavioral symptoms.

Response by Senate Committee members for Homeland Security and Government Affairs toward the United States Government Accountability Office (GAO) report is alarming. The December 2011 GAO Child Foster Care drug audit report uncovered excessive and abusive prescribing of ADHD stimulant and psychiatric medications to children within the child foster care system. The rush by physicians to prematurely prescribe must be reviewed and reformed by their respective medical governing bodies to avoid unnecessary deaths of children in America as well as other countries. The United States leads the world with over 120,000 annual deaths due to overall adverse drug reactions, including overmedicating, which makes this statistic the third leading cause of death after cardiac disease and cancer.

Parents, educators, and healthcare professionals will acquire new knowledge to make informed decisions regarding comprehensive clinical assessments and treatment plans in children battling behavioral symptoms. As author of *The American Epidemic*, and over twenty-five years of consultative pharmacy experience specializing in ADHD and psychiatric medications, the new clinical assessment recommendations for alternative treatment plans to prevent overmedicating our youth will be revealed. Solutions for America's epidemic shall be discussed through a step by step Action Plan for Childhood Behavioral Conditions to help parents.... help their children determine cause of behavioral symptoms prior to premature drug therapy, and reverse a powerful system that is...

Over Medicating Our Youth

CHAPTER I

The Family Unit

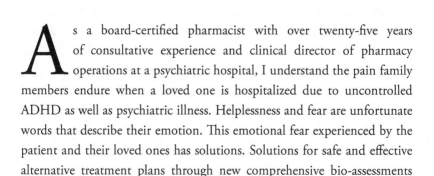

A s a board-certified pharmacist with over twenty-five years of consultative experience and clinical director of pharmacy operations at a psychiatric hospital, I understand the pain family members endure when a loved one is hospitalized due to uncontrolled ADHD as well as psychiatric illness. Helplessness and fear are unfortunate words that describe their emotion. This emotional fear experienced by the patient and their loved ones has solutions. Solutions for safe and effective alternative treatment plans through new comprehensive bio-assessments for ADHD and psychiatric behavioral symptoms prior to prematurely medicating our youth will be discussed.

There are definable risk factors contributing to the onset of childhood behavioral symptoms. Parents, educators, and healthcare professionals realize that premature drug treatment of symptoms is no longer the prudent course of action. Over 78 percent of adult psychiatric patients admitted to my adult psychiatric hospital have a comorbidity diagnosis, including diabetes, heart disease and most importantly some form of digestive nutritional dysfunction. The discussion in later chapters regarding new solutions for assessment of children especially for digestive and nutritional dysfunction will give parents, educators as well as physicians knowledge as to the cause of behavioral symptoms, including ADHD, autism as well as addictive behaviors. New bio-assessments used in successful treatment plans, thereby reversing the overmedicating trend in childhood behavioral development shall be clearly discussed.

The family unit environment should be the first of many assessments, if a child exhibits chronic behavioral symptoms. Before a loved one's psychological behavioral condition reaches the crisis state involving hospitalization, parents, educators, and physicians should realize the importance of the family unit and how it relates to childhood behavioral development. Many risk factors effect behavioral development, however the family unit environment functions as a primary source of stability for child behavior.

The family unit is unique. The diversity in family units across America may offer insight into the behavioral challenges many children face during their developmental growth. These challenges have escalated during the past fifteen years. Parents are faced with more adversity and stress in today's America. Economic decline of the average American family is pervasive. Dual-parent income is now mandatory to keep family units financially solvent. Parents' time spent with their children on a daily basis is on a significant decline. Negative peer pressure affecting the family unit is pervasive.

Many case studies reveal that family unit risk factors may lead to the onset of certain forms of ADHD as well as psychiatric behavior. Although the family unit environment is only one risk factor in the causation of behavioral symptoms, a thorough evaluation should be immediately considered.

One study was reviewed from the Archives of General Psychiatry, entitled "Family-Environment Risk Factors for Attention Deficit Hyperactivity Disorder. A Test of Rutter's Indicators of Adversity."

Background: This study investigated whether family environment risk factors are associated with Attention Deficit Hyperactivity Disorder (ADHD). Compelling work by Rutter and co-workers' revealed that it was the aggregate of adversity factors (parental criminality, maternal mental disorder, severe marital discord, and foster care placement) rather than the presence of any single factor that leads to impaired development. Based on the work of Rutter, we hypothesized a positive association between indicators of adversity and diagnosis of ADHD and ADHD-associated impairments.

Methods: We studied 140 ADHD and 120 normal subjects. Subjects were non- Hispanic white males between ages of six and seventeen years. Rutter's indicators of adversity were used to predict ADHD-related psychopathology as well as impaired cognitive and psychosocial functioning.

Results: The odds for the ratio for the diagnosis of ADHD increased as the number of Rutter's adversity index predicted ADHD-related psychopathology (depression, anxiety, and conduct disorder), learning disabilities, cognitive impairment, and psychosocial dysfunction.

Conclusions: A positive association appears to exist between adversity indicators and the risk for ADHD as well as for its associated psychiatric, cognitive, and psychosocial impairments. These findings stress the importance of adverse family-environment variables as risk factors for children with ADHD.

PMID: 7771916 (PubMed-indexed for MEDLINE)[1]

Unfortunately, the current primary treatment interventions for behavioral challenges in children involve prematurely medicating our youth prior to ruling out underlying causation through multiple assessments, including the family unit.

I would like to offer a brief glimpse into my family unit and my world of parenting prior to the discussion of bio-assessments and solutions to reverse the Childhood Behavioral Health Crisis in America afflicting our child and young adult population. This crisis requires immediate intervention to help parents help their children determine cause of behavioral challenges prior to premature drug therapy. Intervention to preserve the family unit is more difficult today than ever before in American history. Raising six children ages twenty-three, nineteen, eighteen, seventeen, fifteen and twelve is not easy and, in today's world, can be the most challenging and worthwhile job a parent will ever face. I liken it to riding a roller coaster . . . There are many emotional highs and lows to address on a weekly basis. Parenting can be difficult, and sometimes will test your resolve to remain patient. The weekly drama of raising five daughters has many twists and turns, ups and downs. Over the years, many potential crisis situations involving our teenage daughters have been mitigated because of parental involvement. The ability to listen and communicate with our children has given us a blessing with six children who truly value the importance of the family unit.

Robert, age twenty-three, is the leader of his five younger sibling sisters. He was encouraged at age nine to find a hobby that he truly enjoyed. A year of soccer and a year of basketball proved not to be exciting. Eventually, one hobby took him on a journey across the United States. His true love of travel ice hockey dominated his sense of being. Robert had many friends in high school. There was only one true lifelong friend, however. His name was Jeremiah. Jeremiah focused on his great running abilities in track. They were clones, both striving for excellence in different athletics. They exhibited true friendship and respected each other's athletic endeavors. Their high school years were filled with great memories and life experiences.

Jeremiah and Robert went separate collegiate ways in hopes to fulfill their lifelong dream in college athletics. Jeremiah was a saint sent from a divine spirit. He was taken from this earth on November 11, 2011 for a cause.....a cause to make people around the world realize that the current system of assessing and treating patients with behavioral symptoms requires immediate reform. His battle with bipolar disease, like many thousands of children and young adults, took a rapid turn for the worse after his nineteenth birthday.

Jeremiah was not given a voice to help determine the cause of his bipolar symptoms. His closed head injury from early childhood, as I discuss in later chapters, was never aggressively treated and appropriately monitored. Powerful atypical antipsychotic and antidepressant medications became his only option, sending him into a rapid downward spiral.

Jeremiah accomplished more spiritual development in his twenty years than most people would develop in a lifetime. His laughter and positive presence filled the room no matter where he went. Hope and vision were just two salient traits. With positive loving support from his parents during his childhood, Jeremiah was a great united leader of his peers, bringing all kids his age together from diverse backgrounds. Drama was not in Jeremiah's or Robert's repertoire. They sincerely enjoyed talking about their lifetime goals and ambitions. When Jeremiah transferred to Robert's high school, they immediately became close friends. They were both made from the same mold of athletic discipline and the desire to excel in their different athletic pathways.

Throughout Robert's high school years, hockey took him to exciting places on the East coast, Midwest, and even Wyoming, where he played his Junior (A) hockey season prior to making his ultimate dream come true. In September 2010, his dream of becoming an NCAA Division I college goaltender became reality, while Jeremiah obtained a full-ride college scholarship in track.

My objective as a first-time parent in 1990 was to patiently encourage our first-born child to become a positive role model for his siblings while my wife and I provided a caring home environment. Robert helped guide our family unit toward a positive childhood behavioral development path. This requires years of patience and sacrifice by a parent to help ensure positive development occurs. No matter what the socioeconomic background a child faces, positive childhood behavioral development is possible. The parent is responsible to help guide this development.

At times, I recall becoming frustrated at my son's lack of interest in certain extracurricular activities to keep him busy. This frustration can become a negative factor in parenting. The main objective as a parent is not let this frustration overcome your ability to listen to your child and effectively channel their energies toward their true passion. Do not let your own desires suffocate your child's desires.

A very good friend of mine, Emmanuel, is a father who immigrated to the United States from Ghana. He has similar views regarding positive child development in the United States as well as less modernized countries such as Ghana. He views the United States as a country with unlimited opportunities for positive childhood behavioral development.

However, he also believes that children between the ages of four and eighteen have more distractions, which negatively impacts their focus toward positive behavioral development. Emmanuel believes that children in less developed countries around the world can be more successful at achieving positive behavioral development.

In many regions of Ghana, for example, children are required at a very early age to focus on the immediate needs of the family. This builds positive character, including self-reliance, self- confidence, and self-esteem for the child. Emmanuel states "Children in less developed countries, like Ghana, listen and obey their parents and educators as a rule. There is no tolerance for disrespect." The culture in specific regions of Ghana is very demanding toward children. While growing up in Ghana, children had to complete multiple chores before heading off to school. The school day was filled with constant learning exercises. Disruption in the classroom was not tolerated due to strict reverence for the instructor. If a child were to disobey, strict discipline to the child was immediate and effective to prevent future disruptions. Behavioral disruptions by children in the classroom begin with behavioral disruptions in the home.

This is not to say that children are not allowed to express themselves while having fun with their peers and siblings. However, boundaries are set by parents and school systems for children to respect, as they proceed through their childhood behavioral development. Currently, these boundaries set by parents and school systems in the United States are not respected by children to the extent they were decades ago. The problem in today's America is that parents are often given a free pass by our government when they fail to effectively guide their family unit.

This negative trend in parenting has escalated during the last fifteen years. Eventually, the family unit erodes due to extreme negative circumstances, and many children are forced into temporary foster care. Currently, there are over 420,000 children trapped in the foster care system primarily due to parental neglect and abuse. This cycle must be drastically curtailed due to the fact that children in the foster care system, funded by American taxpayers, are being prematurely overmedicated with ADHD stimulant amphetamine and psychiatric medications, according to data obtained by the United States Government Accountability Office (GAO) 2011 Child Foster Care report, which will be discussed extensively in later chapters.

My daughters Nikki, Brittany, Brooke, Marissa, and Katelyn Rose are social butterflies. They have their individual hobbies and love to be around their friends. Nikki is extremely good at fashion design and marketing. Her goal is to become a fashion industry expert in Chicago or New York City after college. Brittany is also a college student and aspires to become a physician assistant. Brooke plays the piano and participates in studio dance. Marissa also plays the piano and competes in cross country track and lacrosse. Katelyn Rose competes in cross country track and competes in dance. All of our daughters have big hearts and enjoy being around their peers. Because of parental patience and understanding, our daughters exhibit a true and sincere character among their peers.

The memories of our daughters' year-to-year development are treasures they will never truly understand until they, one day, have children of their own. Sure, we had our share of girl drama and "teenager vs. parent battles" throughout the years, but they always knew that their parents loved them more than anything in the world.

Sincere and unconditional love given to a child, even during time of tumultuous "teenager vs. parent battles," is just one critical element to ensure positive childhood behavior and family unit development. This mutual love, respect, and communication between a child and their parents is essential to overcome teenage peer pressure.

My wish to all my daughters is that they emulate their mother by raising their future children with unconditional love and respect. Unconditional love for a child can bridge gaps in communication that has become an identifiable risk factor in childhood behavioral development in teenagers. Our daughters' big hearts and respect for others come from many hours of parental leadership from my wife and I.

Over the years, my wife and I have kept our children very busy with activities during their youth and through high school. They are always on the go. The book calendar of events in our kitchen is the size of Mount Everest. Honestly, I do not know how my wife has kept track of events over the years.

According to the Mayo Clinic Study, the average time a parent spends with their child has decreased by twelve hours a week since 1960. In a recent survey asking teenagers a simple question "What do your parents do to show they love you?" three of the most popular answers were related:

1. "They spend time with me"
2. "They take time out of their busy schedules"
3. "They talk to me when I have a problem" [2]

Parents should realize the value and reward of investing time with their children, especially during the teenage years to combat peer pressure. In the United States, teenage peer pressure has impacted the success of the family unit resulting in negative child behavioral development. Peer pressure may effectively be eliminated by keeping a child focused and active, rather than becoming distracted or reactive to the negative effects that peer pressure may create.

As children develop into their teenage years, peer pressure plays a greater role in life. School activities and functions take them away from home for longer periods of time. Family time with parents and siblings becomes less and sometimes peers may seem like part of your extended family. If appropriately monitored by parents, peers can actually be a positive influence for behavioral development. Encouragement and social connectivity are very important aspects involved in childhood behavioral development. Peers with positive character and integrity can actually encourage you to work harder toward achieving goals.

On the other hand, peers with no character and discipline can negatively affect childhood behavioral development. These negative effects invariably lead to a lack of self- image, self-confidence as well as self-esteem resulting in poor childhood behavioral development. Negative self-image in a child may perpetuate and may contribute to erosion of the family unit. However, there are many techniques to help children increase their self-image and emotional thought process as discussed in chapter 3.

Additionally, the advancement of technology has affected behavioral development, if not appropriately monitored by the parent. These advancements include cellular phones, text messaging, and online book profiles. For example, chronic text messaging over a short period can impinge nerve flow from the cervical spine due to the head being protruded forward and in a down position. Blocked nervous system energy flow is a contributing factor in the onset of teenage behavioral symptoms. Cell phones should not be allowed in the classroom since they contribute to the onset of behavioral symptoms in the following way:

- Decreased attention and focus in the classroom: The communication between teenagers continues in the classroom through texting. Concentration to the lesson is diminished as well as the child's ability to strengthen cognitive function.
- Sleep pattern disturbance: Teenagers typically keep their cell phones by their beds at night. This could create an anxiety problem over a period of time leading to interrupted sleep.
- Lack of communication skills: Texting will make a child believe that they need to be accessible at an instant moment. This creates in inability to ignore outside communication. Therefore, effective communication person to person becomes diminished due to lack of focused attention.

Other factors affecting positive behavioral development involve teenage drug abuse, including opiate addiction which is another epidemic in America. Opiate prescription medications including Vicodin and Oxycontin are more plentiful today on high school as well as college campuses than ever before in American history. Teenagers and young adults should understand the addictive properties of these two most popular opiate drugs. Once a prescription opiate addiction begins, the risk factor to develop heroin addiction is magnified.

Parents should not underestimate the negative impact teenage drug abuse has toward positive behavioral development and the family unit. These drugs include excessive consumption of alcohol and marijuana in conjunction with ADHD stimulant as well as psychiatric medications which may lead to a higher risk of addictive behaviors. The opiate addiction epidemic stems from negative peer pressure as well as the rise in ADHD stimulants, antidepressants, and antianxiety medications that many young children are legally prescribed to correct behavioral symptoms prior to ruling out risk factors.

Additionally, the new challenge for parents and school systems in America involve the legal teenager Marijuana Medical Card. Teenagers are acquiring legal marijuana cards from physicians in many instances without a legitimate and chronic end-stage pain management diagnosis. This alarming trend is fueling the childhood behavioral health crisis. Parents, educators as well as healthcare professionals should understand the increased health risks when a teenage child consumes marijuana in conjunction with other prescribed medications including ADHD stimulants and psychoactive drugs.

Establishing and developing a successful family unit is difficult for two parents, let alone one. Parents must have full control of the family unit by enforcing boundaries for their children as they approach teenage behavioral development. The family unit is one of the most powerful and influential forces that will guide the behavioral development of our youth. Preservation of the family unit, wherein all members have mutual respect for one another, is paramount to maintaining positive growth and development.

While raising six children, my wife and I are frequently tested by blips of disrespect from our teenagers. Over the years, we manage to keep parental focus by choosing only the major teenage battles of engagement. During the course of parenting, teenager battles will come and go. The important parental statement at the end of the day is to tell our kids "I love you."

Throughout American history, success of the family unit has endured many challenges. Escalating divorce rates during the last decade have contributed to the breakdown of the family unit, making it more difficult to achieve positive childhood behavioral development. However, many children from blended families have adapted to change and are able to achieve positive behavioral development due to strong, positive parental influence. Many blended families are actually stronger in providing an environment of positive behavioral development due to parents encouraging supportive interaction with their new step siblings.

Most importantly, foster care children and their foster parents are extremely challenged to achieve a successful family unit for positive childhood behavioral growth. Over fifty percent of foster kids in the United States are prescribed psychiatric and ADHD stimulant drugs. Many foster care children are overprescribed and overmedicated with multiple unlabeled psychiatric uses from physicians who do not prescribe prudent medication therapies.

The United States Government Accountability Office 2011 Child Foster Care drug audit report investigated the use of these expensive drugs in children of foster care families. The results were alarming. Not only were these expensive drugs paid by state Medicaid programs funded by American taxpayers, many psychiatrists across the country were using potentially deadly drug combinations for symptoms that were not FDA approved as safe and effective in the child population.

How can a child within the foster care system have a chance at achieving positive behavioral development if he or she is medicated with potentially harmful drugs prior to ruling out nutritional, physiological and environmental risk factors for the cause of their symptoms?

Solutions for positive behavioral development in America for all children, including those victimized within the foster care system, is possible. Identifying the cause of behavioral symptoms prior to prematurely medicating children will unite leaders in America. Leaders in public health policy, parenting, education as well as all healthcare professions will help reform the process of assessing behavioral symptoms, thereby creating a platform to strengthen the family unit for positive childhood behavioral development.

The non-profit Coalition Against Over Medicating Our Youth (CAOOY) is leading a strong movement to help parents help their children. CAOOY invites people from all walks of life, nationally and internationally....become actively engaged in the process to mandate change in the assessment process, especially young children battling behavioral symptoms. The Action Plan for Childhood Behavioral Conditions provides a template for the new assessment process. You are encouraged to take notes, and "Ask the Pharmacist", as new assessments helping children with behavioral challenges are here, preventing a system that is overmedicating our youth.

Notes

_____

_____

_____

_____

_____

_____

_____

_____

_____

_____

_____

_____

_____

_____

_____

_____

_____

_____

_____

_____

_____

_____

Ask the Pharmacist • www.CAOOY.org

Helping Determine Causation
of Behavioral Conditions

Donations Provide
Free Clinical Bio-Assesment
and Medication Consultations

CAOOY
Coalition Against Overmedicating Our Youth
WORLD   ADVOCATE   FOR   CHILDREN©

CHAPTER 2

Evolution of the Behavioral Health Crisis in America

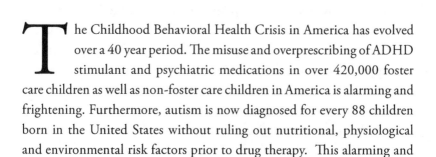

T he Childhood Behavioral Health Crisis in America has evolved over a 40 year period. The misuse and overprescribing of ADHD stimulant and psychiatric medications in over 420,000 foster care children as well as non-foster care children in America is alarming and frightening. Furthermore, autism is now diagnosed for every 88 children born in the United States without ruling out nutritional, physiological and environmental risk factors prior to drug therapy. This alarming and frightening trend will jeopardize the viability of our next generation, if not reversed by implementing new mandatory assessment protocols in young children.

The United States Government Accountability Office Child Foster Care report of December 2011 proves that reform in the assessment and treatment process of children exhibiting behavioral symptoms is mandatory to ensure the health and wellbeing of our next generation. The long-term side effects of powerful ADHD stimulant amphetamine and psychiatric medications in children are now known. Furthermore, the pharmaceutical and political alliance created in 1995 in the State of Texas contributed to The Childhood Behavioral Health Crisis, as special investigator for Pennsylvania's Office of Inspector General, Allen Jones as well as State Attorney Generals reveal.

Many institutions of psychiatry are realizing that a personalized diagnosis and treatment should be the new mandate in America to solve the childhood behavioral health crisis. Johns Hopkins Department of Psychiatry and Behavioral Sciences advocates this philosophy in the treatment of behavioral conditions. Johns Hopkins School of Medicine is ranked number one in psychiatry and behavioral health sciences in the United States by the U.S. World News Report. Since 1980, Johns Hopkins University Department of Psychiatry has steadfastly viewed the Diagnostic and Statistical Manual (DSM) of Mental Disorders, which is the bible of psychiatric diagnosing, as fundamentally flawed, according to Johns Hopkins Reflections on Clinical Excellence.

According to Professor Margaret Chisolm, MD, at Johns Hopkins University, "we have witnessed the harmful effects of the ascendancy of the DSM on our field, including the creation of a generation of psychiatrists who no longer routinely conduct a thorough psychiatric evaluation for each patient. It's now a rare psychiatrist who takes stock of an individual's life story, intelligence, temperament, and behaviors before reducing the origin of the patient's complaint to brain disease."

Dr. Chisolm adequately describes what is necessary for treating children with behavioral conditions, "At, Hopkins, we have remained committed to measured, systematic approach to the psychiatric evaluation of each and every patient. Although we recognize the time-consuming nature of such an evaluation, we also know that it's essential to the practice of psychiatry".[3]

The failure to comprehensively assess children and young adults for the cause of behavioral challenges may have dire consequences involving long term stimulant drug therapy. Years ago, as a practicing community retail pharmacist, I was frantically called by the mother of a seventeen-year-old patient for advice. Her son was taking Ritalin (methylphenidate) since the age of seven. Initially, his grades improved dramatically while his hyperactivity disorder, due to an ADHD diagnosis, ceased. With no major side effects, except occasional drowsiness, during the course of his treatment, she explained to me that she took him off the medication prior to him attending college. She no longer wanted her son taking the drug. Over a one-week period, she gradually took him off the drug. It was the eighth day that I received her frantic call. She explained that her son's lower right extremity went numb for over a day with no improvement. I told her that since her son was on Ritalin over a long period of time that one week withdrawal was not adequate. I informed her to immediately take her son to the emergency room for further testing to rule out irreversible vascular system damage. Upon re-administering Ritalin, the teenager's side effects diminished. This case study shows the addictive nature of methylphenidate which may cause life-threatening vascular withdrawal symptoms. Furthermore, Ritalin and cocaine act on the same receptor cites in the brain. This biochemical fact explains why Ritalin, or any ADHD stimulant, should not be underestimated for physical and psychological addictive side effects.

The long-term side effects of ADHD stimulant as well as psychiatric drugs in children are now known. There is factual data that long-term powerful amphetamine stimulant drug use in humans may lead to long-term cardiovascular complications as well as the onset of anxiety, minor depression as well as major depression, according to data released in the FDA Med Guide Alert warning system. Although the short term effects of ADHD stimulant medications including Adderall, Ritalin, Vyvanse, Focalin, Metadate and Concerta may provide a positive cognitive response, parents should understand that the long term behavioral side effects may become possible. Therefore, determining the cause of behavioral symptoms as discussed in the Action Plan for Childhood Behavioral Conditions should be completed prior to drug therapy intervention.

For over forty years, the psychiatric drug manufacturing industry has inundated educators, parents, physicians, and policymakers with misinformation that ADHD as well as psychiatric conditions can be treated only with drug therapy. Does this industry have a child's "health" in mind or is it the "wealth" created by targeting excessive and dangerous drug use with deficient monitoring protocols in young foster care and non-foster care children?

The late 1980s was the advent of "new psychopharmacology" created by a relationship between the American Psychiatric Association (APA) and the psychiatric drug manufacturing industry. This partnership also solidified the notion that the ADHD diagnosis is considered a mental health illness in accordance with the Diagnostic and Statistical Manual of Mental Disorders. Many parents in America are shocked that a diagnosis of ADHD is a diagnosis of mental illness.

In 1987, the psychiatric drug manufacturing industry recorded annual revenue of approximately one-half billion dollars from ADHD and psychiatric medications. By the end of 2011, annual revenue exceeded one hundred billion dollars, with the greatest percent increase in consumption involving children four to twenty-two years of age. Children in the United States are prescribed over three times as many ADHD stimulant and psychiatric medications, than the rest of the world's children combined, according to data collected by Scientific American.[4]

Millions of parents across America are faced with the decision to medicate their children exhibiting behavioral symptoms, including ADHD and autism. This decision can become one of the most difficult choices parents have to make during critical behavioral development years. Information as to cause of symptoms should be fully reviewed by parents, physicians, therapists, as well as educators prior to drug therapy intervention.

Although short-term response to drug therapy may provide resolution of symptoms, the long-term side effects of drug therapy should be considered and re-evaluated. Alternative assessment protocols to determine cause of symptoms should be implemented before a final treatment plan is implemented. The Food and Drug Administration (FDA) has mandated Med Guide alerts for all ADHD stimulant and psychiatric medications in children as well as adults. Possible long-term side effects involving anxiety, depression as well as cardiovascular disease, are also a required WARNING in the FDA Med Guide alert.

As a young child starts and continues to consume ADHD stimulant medications including Ritalin, Focalin, Adderall, Vyvanse, Concerta, and Metadate for an extended period of time, symptoms of the behavioral condition may worsen and potentially lead to general depression or a more severe form of depression called bipolar (mania) depression, according to the FDA Med Guide alert.

Mania or bipolar behavior may manifest itself in the following manner:

1. Feeling overly happy, excited, or confident
2. Feeling extremely irritable, aggressive, and wired
3. Having uncontrollable racing thoughts
4. Thinking of yourself as overly important, gifted, or special
5. Making poor judgments as in relationships and money
6. Engaging in risky behavior or taking more risks than normal [5]

Since 1995, the number of children diagnosed with bipolar depression increased by forty-fold to over eight hundred thousand children during a ten year period. Additionally, over seven million children in the United States are diagnosed and prescribed stimulant ADHD medications. More disturbing is the fact that over fifty percent of foster care children in the United States are prescribed multiple combinations of psychiatric medications and ADHD stimulant medications. [6] Currently, over 12 million children and young adults in the United States are prescribed ADHD stimulant or psychiatric medications.

Further cause of alarm in childhood medication safety involves the prescribing of powerful atypical psychiatric medications including Risperdal, Haldol, Abilify, Geodon, Zyprexa, Saphris, Seroquel, Clozaril, Latuda, Fanapt, and Invega. Over a decade ago, these powerful psychiatric drug compounds were prescribed only for severe mentally ill patients. Now, the psychiatric drug industry has lobbied, in the name of health wealth, to psychiatrists in America as well as internationally for the purpose of prescribing psychiatric medications as early as the age of one, according to data collected by the United States Government Accountability Office Child Foster Care report of 2011.

This drug cycle began in school systems within forty-three states via the Teen Screen program. This program was designed by a professor of child psychiatry at Columbia who served as a paid consultant for GlaxoSmithKline, as well as other psychiatric drug manufacturers. This psychiatrist was also one of the principal developers of the discredited Diagnostic and Statistical Manual of Mental Disorders.

The intent of the Teen Screen program was to ask teens simple behavioral questions and, depending on their overall score, be referred to social workers or psychiatrists for further evaluation. Once referred and placed into drug therapy as the only option, many parents were unaware that their child becomes trapped in the Diagnostic and Statistical Manual (DSM) criteria for mental illness.

Although the Teen Screen programs were designed to identify and prevent psychiatric conditions from worsening, exacerbation of teenage psychiatric behavior is more prominent today than fifteen years ago due to premature drug therapy, prior to determining cause or etiology of the symptoms. Treatment by a highly qualified therapist should be the first form of intervention for childhood behavioral symptoms, followed by a reputable physician specializing in behavioral conditions to rule out medical risk factors causing the symptoms.

Programs similar to Teen Screen are a direct cause of the Behavioral Health Crisis in America afflicting our youth. While the intent to screen children for mental illness is justified as a preventative health-care measure, parental informed consent and alternative assessment as well as treatment plans are not aggressively followed prior to prematurely medicating children. Additionally, this process violates a child's human rights due to breach of informed consent.

Currently, high schools across America are developing and implementing peer to peer mental health screening programs to prevent escalating teen suicide rates in high schools. These types of programs are well intended to make students aware that they have people to talk about their behavioral problems. However, students should understand their right to have comprehensive assessments to rule out nutritional, physiological and environmental risk factors as well as behavioral talk therapy prior to premature drug therapy.

John W. Whitehead, president and founder of the Rutherford Institute, is very critical of schools that implement this type of program. He states

"Parents need to understand that there are some immediate steps which can be taken to combat the increasing problem of government encroaching into the privacy of the family. First, it is critical to learn your rights as a parent. Second, contact your local school officials and demand that you be notified immediately if they are planning to conduct mental health screening on your children. Finally, follow Rhoades' example and fight back against this encroachment on parental rights".[7]

Since suicide is the second leading cause of death in the United States college student population, parents should also be very proactive with their children once they reach the age of eighteen. If your child has a noticeable behavior change that is affecting their health, parents should help them seek therapy as well as obtain a differential diagnosis for cause of the behavioral symptoms.

To prevent a behavioral crisis, this process should occur after the parent obtains guardian rights for their child prior to age eighteen. Failure to obtain rights for an eighteen-year-old child with severe psychological crisis behavior will not allow a parent to obtain informed consent rights for their child's treatment plan. In other words, a psychiatrist can legally refuse parental requests for alternative assessment and treatment plan options.

While Mr. David Oaks, director of MindFreedom International, states "I see an amazing rebellion stirring that cuts across usual political lines. A federal bureaucrat recently called this a 'curious coalition' in the media. We are seeing traditionally conservative groups working together with progressive social justice and libertarian groups. The psychiatric drug companies have overextended themselves, and the general public is showing signs of waking up. I just hope they wake up soon!"[8]

In response to national as well as international global teen screening, Vera Sharav of the Alliance for Human Research Protection states "This dubious initiative is a radical invasion of privacy, leaving no room for individual choice . . . or the freedom for parents to say no to psychotropic drugs for their children."

According to Jan Eastgate, president of the Citizens Commission on Human Rights (CCHR) states, "Children worldwide are under extremely dangerous assault. Parents and teachers are also deceived in the name of better mental health and better education. The CCHR report is devastating:

1. In the United States alone, 1.5 million children on antidepressants are at risk of known, drug-induced violent or suicidal effects.
2. Education achievement standards in public schools have plummeted as a result of psychology-based education curricula.
3. Since the 1960s, the violent crime rate for under age eighteen in the United States increased by more than 147 percent and for drug abuse violations over 2,900 percent.

CCHR is committed to the idea that it is through the legacy of our children that societies survive or fail. The CCHR report is written to enlighten those parents who work sincerely and diligently in the hope of guaranteeing their children a better education and a greater hope for success in life. It is for dedicated teachers who also work for the love of children and their well-being. In fact, this report is for anyone who instinctively understands that children not only need love and protection, and are at all times precious, but also that they represent new life today, and, most importantly, new life tomorrow".[9]

Citizens Commission on Human Rights is the largest worldwide watchdog commission regarding safe and prudent use of psychiatric therapy in children as well as adults. They are not anti-psychiatry; rather they advocate alternative interventions prior to prematurely placing children on powerful ADHD stimulant and psychiatric medications.

Alternative treatment interventions may involve extensive therapy with specialists in psychotherapy, bio-energy feedback, brain wave optimization and therapists who help people empower the subconscious mind toward healing, while a medical doctor safely and effectively monitors the entire progress of the child's treatment plan by ruling out nutritional, physiological, and environmental risk factors causing the behavioral symptoms. Alternative treatment plans are the positive result of differential diagnosing, which prevents a child from being prematurely medicated since multiple clinicians are involved in the assessment and treatment, if medication therapy is warranted.

Many psychiatric patient records are highlighted with a "provisional diagnosis," meaning the psychiatrist is not sure what the actual diagnosis is due to a lack of information. However, a differential diagnosis refers to more than one possibility and a differentiation is required prior to drug treatment. Differential diagnosing assessed by an independent medical doctor is critical prior to medicating a child with ADHD stimulant or psychoactive medications by a psychiatrist or pediatrician. Physicians should rule out all possible causes or etiology of the behavioral condition prior to implementing a drug treatment plan.

Parents, educators and healthcare professionals concerned about the assessment as well as treatment options for childhood behavioral symptoms should be aware of recent history in the drug manufacturing and relationships with state mental health programs. Before one can ask why the vast majority of psychiatrists in America do not refer a child for a differential diagnosis to determine cause of symptoms prior to prescribing psychiatric medications, the answer can be found historically in April 2002.

The highly publicized and disputatious New Freedom Commission on Mental Health was established to study mental health services and provide recommendations in an attempt to allow access to all Americans to mental health treatment. This commission identified areas of improvement to allow access of care for adults and children with severe mental illness. The intent of this commission appeared noble. However, the truth involved access for all patients, including children, to the most expensive psychoactive medications for the purpose of chemical behavioral control by psychiatrists, as special investigators and multiple state attorney generals prove. Further support of the opposition argument lies in the origin of the commission.

The Texas Medication Algorithm Project (TMAP) was created in Texas in 1995. This project was the coalition of individuals from the University of Texas, psychiatrists, pharmaceutical manufacturing industry, and the mental health system of Texas. Through formidable alliances they advised the use of newer and more expensive psychiatric medications to state psychiatric hospitals, prison systems, and the foster care system.

Public awareness and opposition to this alliance was made by Mr. Allen Jones, former investigator in the Pennsylvania Office of Inspector General (OIG), Bureau of Special Investigations. He stated that there were not conclusive medical studies proving that the new expensive drugs were any more effective than the older generics already on the market. Mr. Jones wrote a lengthy report in which he stated that behind the recommendation of the New Freedom Commission was the "political/pharmaceutical alliance."

This alliance, according to investigator Allen Jones, was responsible for creating the TMAP, which promoted the use of newer more expensive psychiatric medications, without justifiable clinical benefit to patients within the state Medicaid program. He further claimed that the initiative of the TMAP was to implement a comprehensive national policy, and treat mental illness with expensive patented medications of questionable benefit, deadly side effects, forcing private insurers as well as Medicaid/Medicare to provide payment. Opponents of the New Freedom Commission did not believe the benefits of the plan, except increased profits for the psychiatric drug manufacturing corporations and psychiatrists.[10]

Additionally, opponents of the New Freedom Commission had grave concerns regarding the potential side effects of these medications in the child population including increased substance abuse, drug dependence, and metabolic dysfunction. Parents, educators, physicians, and policymakers should be aware that once a child starts ADHD stimulant or psychiatric drug therapy, there is a very high probability that more medications will be added on and withdrawal of these medications becomes very difficult. The drug abuse potential in children may increase as they approach their late teenage years, since they have been behaviorally modified to believe that drugs are a necessary part of their existence.

The manner in which our society assesses, diagnoses, and ultimately treats children with behavioral symptoms requires significant reform. Parents, educators, and all healthcare professionals should fully understand the implications of the court case against Johnson & Johnson, the largest health-care product company in the world. This case epitomizes the "culture of medical mental health treatment" in our children. This case against Johnson & Johnson and their pharmaceutical subsidiary Janssen pharmaceutical corporation mandates a change in childhood psychiatric care. This case represents one of the reasons American children consume three times the amount of psychiatric medications than the world's children combined.

On January 20, 2012, Johnson & Johnson agreed to pay a 158-million-dollar settlement to the State of Texas and former special bureau investigator, Allen Jones, who was wrongfully fired for exposing fraudulent marketing activities within the pharmaceutical drug manufacturing industry in association with the TMAP. The case is called State of Texas ex. rel. Jones vs. Janssen LP, D-1GV-04-001288, in District Court, Travis County, Austin, Texas. This suit accuses the drug maker of inappropriately marketing the antipsychotic brand name drug, Risperdal, to state recipients of the Medicaid program for the poor. Attorneys for the State of Texas stated in their suit that Johnson & Johnson fraudulently promoted Risperdal as well as overcharged Medicaid over 579 million dollars from 1994 to 2008.

The grand jury received testimony involving Johnson & Johnson's pharmaceutical unit, Janssen, paying the Mental Health Director of Texas since 1999 to recommend the expensive Risperdal brand as a first-choice option. Janssen also paid this director to fly around the country to influence the development of the TMAP in other state Medicaid programs. The State of Texas lawsuit also charged that Janssen defrauded the state Medicaid program by fraudulently promoting Risperdal for uses not approved by the FDA, including children with psychiatric disorders. Additionally, a Texas Medicaid investigator stated in testimony, that the Mental Health Director signed several consulting agreements with Janssen while employed with the State of Texas.[11]

The State of Texas ex. rel. Jones vs. Janssen suit is separate from numerous other cases in the United States, which attorneys say will cost Johnson & Johnson billions of dollars to settle out of court. Since 1994 this one atypical antipsychotic drug, Risperdal, earned revenue of thirty-four billion dollars. Many attorneys across America are calling the multistate settlement the largest lawsuit in Texas since the Big Tobacco litigation in the 1990s. According to attorney Tom Melsheimer representing whistle-blower Allen Jones in testimony, "Not only was Risperdal not more effective, its risks' were worse than its competitors, and was forty five times more expensive".[12]

Since Risperdal was FDA approved in 1994, its estimated annual revenue at that time was approximately one billion dollars. The FDA-approved usage was only for "adult" schizophrenia. Upon unethical marketing practices through the TMAP, Risperdal was excessively used in the state's hospitals, prisons, as well as unapproved uses in the child foster care system. Between 1997 and 2010, Risperdal eclipsed revenue of over thirty-four billion dollars.

Even after Risperdal was available in a generic alternative in 2008, fiscal 2010 costs in Texas for brand Risperdal was over fifteen million dollars in comparison with thirteen million dollars for the generic. A question to the current mental health director in Texas is.... why?

State mental health directors should implement a mandatory generic dispensing policy for federally funded taxpayer prescription drug programs. Especially with the aforementioned litigation in Texas, brand Risperdal as well as other branded medication expenditures for all state drug programs should be a fraction of a percent to prevent fraud, waste and abuse.

Allen Jones and attorneys for the State of Texas allege that a process designed to be based on independent experts was co-opted by Janssen using false and misleading information, including ghostwritten articles and industry-funded studies while playing down side effects, including weight gain and diabetes.[13]

The U.S. Justice Department is now investigating the marketing practices of Risperdal according to their filing in August 2011. Johnson & Johnson is expected to plead to a misdemeanor for violating the Food, Drug, and Cosmetic Act as a result of negotiations with the U.S. Securities and Exchange Commission. In a statement by Dr. John David Abramson, health policy expert at Harvard University, he references the Risperdal case as a small example of a larger problem. "Government funded studies regarding the drug's effectiveness were not published until more than a decade after the drug was first approved. We are spending money on a drug that isn't superior and might be inferior to other drugs that cost a fraction as much. It ought to make honest citizens want to throw up to see that this money is being extracted from society for no gain, when our country is headed toward financial ruin." Dr. Abramson helped the state of Louisiana investigate Risperdal for their lawsuit.[14]

Texas Attorney General Medicaid Fraud Division and Allen Jones claim in court proceedings that TMAP is a vehicle to prescribe the most expensive drugs and provide guidelines for the treatment of attention deficit hyperactivity disorder (ADHD), minor depression, bipolar disorder, and ultimately schizophrenia. The FDA mandates Med Guide alerts for all stimulant medications due to their propensity to cause depression with long-term treatment in children.

After special investigator Allen Jones uncovered the waste and abuse regarding drug therapy in 2004, the independent Clinical Antipsychotic Trials of Intervention Effectiveness Study (CATIE) supported his claims. The CATIE study evaluated the effectiveness of the expensive atypical antipsychotic branded drugs including Risperdal, Zyprexa, Seroquel, and Geodon with the older generic antipsychotic generic drug perphenazine (Trilafon). The results overwhelmingly proved that the expensive drug therapies, twelve to fifteen times the cost of perphenazine, did not provide a clinically significant advantage. Upon review of this data in 2005, the TMAP continued to push these expensive drug therapies as primary treatment in children and adults within State Medicaid programs in the United States.

As court documents reveal, Johnson & Johnson Corporation continued to pay the State of Texas director of mental health for expanding the TMAP into other states. Twelve states adopted the TMAP guidelines recommending expensive drug therapies paid by taxpayers instead of lower cost generic alternatives with equivalent efficacy. Within the State of Texas, however, many directors of state-funded community centers and hospitals did not comply with the expensive TMAP mandate from the State of Texas director of mental health. The director of mental health paid two University of Texas professors one hundred thousand dollars to implement a management program for adherence to the TMAP. If individual directors of community centers did not comply with the TMAP mandate, they would lose partial state funding for their facilities.

Eventually, the State of Texas director of mental health was fired on October 9, 2006, due to his role in the TMAP. His firing, ironically, came at the hands of the whistle-blower special investigator Allen Jones lawsuit in 2004. Allen Jones provided state attorneys with damaging evidence of waste and abuse within TMAP guidelines. Upon the recommendation of a special task force, the Texas State Department of Health and Human Services (HHS) reviewed and voted against the TMAP guidelines in 2010.[15]

Public awareness and implications of the State of Texas & Allen Jones lawsuit against Johnson & Johnson is important for children with behavioral conditions. The legal settlement for special investigator Allen Jones and Texas Attorney General Greg Abbott begins a new positive culture in the way behavioral conditions are assessed and ultimately treated in children. Failure of the pharmaceutical industry by fraudulently marketing powerful ADHD stimulant and psychiatric medications for children has financial implications as revealed by the Texas lawsuit decision. Although in some cases behavioral conditions may require the use of these powerful medications for treatment, pharmaceutical manufacturing and retail community pharmacies should take the lead and increase education regarding long term side effects.

The funding authority for all state departments for mental health, United States Department of Health and Human Services (HHS), should recommend state directors adhere to mandatory generic therapies for Medicaid and Medicare recipients. This mandate would eliminate the possibility of collusion in future guideline proposals at the state level. An individualized and comprehensive assessment with alternative therapy interventions prior to prematurely medicating children should become the new mandate for prescribing physicians in America.

The Texas lawsuit against Johnson & Johnson is an example of why physicians should find the cause of behavioral symptoms prior to drug therapy intervention. This new vision of practice will help eliminate the Behavioral Health Crisis afflicting young children. Another example of contributing factors to the Behavioral Health Crisis afflicting America's children involves the five state Government Accountability Office Child Foster Care drug audit under the authority of the United States Congress.

The United States Government Accountability Office presented their report on December 1, 2011, involving a two-year audit of psychiatric and ADHD medications prescribed by psychiatrists for foster care and non-foster care children in the state Medicaid system starting in 2008 through 2010. The data was collected from five geographically diverse states including Michigan, Massachusetts, Oregon, Texas, and Florida. This audit included only 100,000 of the total 420,000 foster care children nationally. State Medicaid payments for ADHD and psychiatric medications prescribed for foster and non-foster children in these five states were as follows:

1. Michigan—$72,749,858
2. Massachusetts—$29,584,901
3. Oregon—$14,326,756
4. Texas—$194,952,105
5. Florida—$64,358,968

Texas spent approximately two hundred million dollars on ADHD and psychiatric medications during this audit period, which represents over fifty percent of all five state's expenditures combined in the drug audit.

Perhaps the opponents of the New Freedom Commission in April 2002 were correct on the commission's purpose of opening the door to children for mental health screening. The important question is what quality of care, did they receive. Additional findings were alarming. Total Michigan Medicaid reimbursement for recipients eighteen years and younger from year 2000 to 2008 for the powerful atypical psychiatric drugs Abilify, Geodon, Risperdal, Seroquel, and Zyprexa went from $1,891,569 to $42,201,804 representing a 2,200 percent increase in expenditure for drugs not FDA approved in children eighteen years old and younger.[16]

Overwhelmingly, Texas led the five states and the nation with foster children receiving up to five times the rate of psychiatric prescribing in comparison with non-foster children. Also foster children in Texas were fifty-three times more likely to be prescribed five or more psychoactive medications at the same time than non-foster children. In Massachusetts, they were nineteen times more likely. In Michigan, the rate was fifteen times. Oregon was thirteen times, while Florida was the lowest rate at four times.[17]

Through multiple interviews with state and federal officials, the investigators related that the increased rates of psychiatric prescribing was due to greater emotional trauma, frequent changes in foster care parents, and state oversight deficiencies. In review of the Government Accountability Office Child Foster Care drug audit report, there was a significant lack of cognitive behavioral therapy (CBT), alternative treatment plans, and differential diagnosing referred by psychiatrists.

A plan of correction eliminating the misuse of ADHD stimulant and psychiatric medications as well as deficient monitoring protocols is mandated to reverse the Behavioral Health Crisis afflicting our youth. During the last twenty years, the political and pharmaceutical alliance contributed to the behavioral health crisis in America involving childhood behavioral development. Additional factors affecting childhood behavioral development must be clearly understood to unite educators, parents, and physicians toward an effective plan of correction. This corrective plan called the Action Plan for Childhood Behavioral Conditions involves a step by step plan that may help parents help their children revert to normal behavior without prematurely overmedicating.

Before drug therapy can be allowed in young children battling behavioral challenges including ADHD and autism, three risk factor classifications for ruling out the cause of symptoms must become the new mandate to protect the health and welfare of our next generation.

Notes

_____

_____

_____

_____

_____

_____

_____

_____

_____

_____

_____

_____

_____

_____

_____

_____

_____

_____

_____

_____

_____

_____

Ask the Pharmacist • www.CAOOY.org

CHAPTER 3

ADHD and Autism Risk Factors

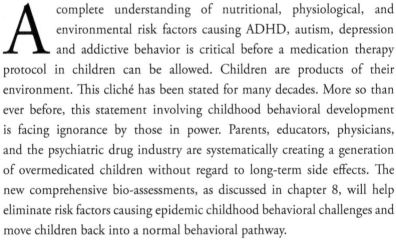

A complete understanding of nutritional, physiological, and environmental risk factors causing ADHD, autism, depression and addictive behavior is critical before a medication therapy protocol in children can be allowed. Children are products of their environment. This cliché has been stated for many decades. More so than ever before, this statement involving childhood behavioral development is facing ignorance by those in power. Parents, educators, physicians, and the psychiatric drug industry are systematically creating a generation of overmedicated children without regard to long-term side effects. The new comprehensive bio-assessments, as discussed in chapter 8, will help eliminate risk factors causing epidemic childhood behavioral challenges and move children back into a normal behavioral pathway.

In the United States, exposure to environmental and nutritional toxins is more prominent today than ever before in American history. Does a child's nutritional and digestive development affect their behavioral development? Many scientific nutritionists prove that childhood nutritional deficiency or mal-absorption will eventually cause chronic and significant cellular oxidation. Ultimately, the child may develop behavioral symptoms as a result to chronic toxin exposure from their environment as well as their food supply. Parents should be vigilant in removing chemically altered food sources from their diet, especially when a child presents psychological, ADHD, autism as well as depressive behavioral symptoms.

The most important health factor involving childhood behavioral development is nutritional absorption and digestive elimination of bodily toxins. The psychiatric drug industry and many psychiatrists believe that nutrition represents a minor cause in the development of behavioral conditions. Countless studies on the effects of poor nutrition prove otherwise. For example, the artificial chemical sweetener, aspartame, is commonly found in over six thousand nutritional products including sugar-free "diet" soft drinks and juices as well as yogurt. This chemically manufactured artificial sweetener metabolizes at a minimum of 90° Fahrenheit in the human body to produce neurotoxins. Furthermore, children do not need large ingested quantities of aspartame to feel the detrimental side effects including:

- behavioral disturbances
- headaches
- visual problems
- memory lapse
- psychological conditions

Children should refrain from any product containing aspartame, especially if they present a behavioral condition. Parents, educators, and physicians should be aware that nutrition plays a critical role in the onset of psychological, ADHD, autistic and depressive symptoms.

Physicians should implement a root cause analysis as outlined in the Action Plan for Childhood Behavioral Conditions prior to placing children on powerful ADHD stimulant or psychiatric medications.

A one- appointment discussion between the patient and physician for behavioral symptoms, especially in the child population, is detrimental. If the nutritional consumption as well as elimination of bodily toxins by the patient is not addressed, and medication is prematurely prescribed, then the child's health is further compromised due to poor nutrition as well as initiating medications for a misdiagnosed patient.

An entire book on the toxic effects of aspartame consumption in children could be written. However, the simple biochemical facts include the following. Aspartame is chemically comprised of three primary compounds including aspartate (40 percent), phenylalanine (50 percent), and methanol (10 percent).

Aspartate is a naturally occurring amino acid, which affects neurotransmission in the brain. Too much aspartate via nutritional intake could cause an increase influx of calcium into neuronal cells creating toxic, highly oxidative, free radical chemical compounds and eventually kills cells critical to positive cognitive behavioral function. This biochemical fact does not happen overnight, however children are very sensitive to this compound if frequently consumed over a period of time.

Phenylalanine is a naturally occurring amino acid and comprises 50 percent of the aspartame chemical sweetener. Phenylalanine, if consumed in large quantities by children, reduces the free circulating neurotransmitter, serotonin, eventually; the child may experience behavioral disturbances including depression or develop a history of seizures.

Alarmingly, the last component of the chemically manufactured sweetener, aspartame, is methanol, also known as wood alcohol. At approximately 90° Fahrenheit, methanol is oxidized in the body to formic acid and formaldehyde. These two toxic compounds are known neurotoxins and may cause behavioral symptoms in children depending on their nutritional consumption of the aspartame sweetener. The Environmental Protection Agency (EPA) limits the oral consumption of methanol to approximately 8 mg per day. The average can of diet soda or juice contains approximately 60 mg of methanol exceeding the limit by a factor of seven. One popular "kid food" containing aspartame is jello. The absorption rate of methanol into the blood is magnified due to the heating process of the jello prior to cooling. Toxic side effects of methanol poisoning in children may include:

- behavioral disturbances
- memory lapse
- depression
- dizziness
- headaches
- visual acuity problems
- numbness in extremities
- chronic fatigue and confusion.

The important fact to note, as a parent, is that aspartame may become a silent causation to abnormal behavioral symptoms. Very early in child development, parents need to take an active role in the elimination of all aspartame-containing food sources as well as chemically processed foods. In doing so, the probability of your child developing behavioral abnormalities will be considerably reduced.

Natural and artificial flavors as well as food colorings may contain chemical compounds similar to aspartame's side effects. Therefore, food sources containing aspartame, as well as natural and artificial flavorings or colorings, should be eliminated from a child's diet. FD & C yellow and red dyes are very common chemical dyes found in many popular foods causing immune suppression as well as behavioral symptoms with long-term consumption.

A team of Dutch researchers at the ADHD Research Center in the Netherlands took one hundred non-medicated children recently diagnosed with ADHD and fed half of the children a diet free of processed foods, chemicals, and allergens. The other half served as a control group. Within five weeks, 64 percent of those children in the test group saw remarkable changes. "After eliminating the dyes and processed foods, they were just normal children with normal behavior," stated lead researcher Dr. Lidy Pelsser. "They were no longer more easily distracted, there were no more forgetful, there were no more temper tantrums." Dr. Pelsser explains, "ADHD is a couple of symptoms-not a disease. There is a paradigm shift needed. If a child is diagnosed ADHD, we should say, okay we got these symptoms, now let use start looking for the cause. With all children we should start with diet research. But now we are giving them all drugs, and that is a huge mistake".[18]

Sixty four percent may seem to be a low percentile response. However, remember that this simple whole foods intervention, eliminating all chemically processed foods as well as gluten from a child's diet, represents only one of many risk factor interventions as discussed in the Action Plan for Childhood Behavioral Conditions.

The following article in the Philly News shows how a celebrity chef dad got his son back on a positive behavioral pathway by incorporating a whole foods diet. Educating his son on the positive health benefits of a whole foods diet proved to be fun and educational at the same time.

BY LAUREN MCCUTCHEON,

Daily News Staff Writer mccutch@phillynews.com, 215-854-5991
Posted: September 06, 2013

That 6-year-old Davin Schulson can make his own lunch (homemade citrusade, chicken tacos and raspberry-watermelon frozen pops) is no surprise. The eldest son of celeb chef-restaurateur Michael Schulson (Center City's Sampan, Atlantic City's Izakaya and Ardmore's The Saint James) has been cooking at his dad's elbow longer than he can remember.

"He was tossing edamame in a pot when he was 18 months old, when we appeared together on 'E! News,' "said his proud papa, also dad to Jordan, 3.

Still, that Davin can stand in one place on a stepladder while single-mindedly squeezing fruit, mixing in maple syrup, loading frozen berries into a blender and then slicing — and sautéing — a chicken breast is somewhat of a miracle.

A year and a half ago, six months before Davin entered kindergarten, at Greenfield Elementary, he, like more than 5 percent of American kids aged 6 to 12, was diagnosed with ADHD.

"He couldn't stay still," said Schulson, who cited Davin's most prominent symptoms of attention deficit hyperactivity disorder as "impulse control." He also exhibited other typical ADHD symptoms of hyperactivity and inattention.

In school, Davin frequently acted out, received daily "red light" warnings about his behavior and eventually had to eat lunch in the principal's office. "His kindergarten teacher had him sit on a [fitness] ball, and he'd just bounce and bounce," recalled the chef.

Schulson took his pre-kindergartener to the Center for Management of ADHD, at the Children's Hospital of Philadelphia, for evaluation. Davin began taking a prescription to control his symptoms.

Schulson, who is divorced and has primary custody of his two kids, wasn't pleased with what he observed in Davin, post-prescription. He described his eldest's medicated state as "in a whole different world." He recalled, "I was like, 'Where's my son?' "

A CURE IN THE KITCHEN?

The chef resolved to find another, drug-free approach. He came upon the Feingold Diet. Born in the 1970s of a West Coast allergist, Feingold is based on the idea that eliminating foods with petroleum-based dyes (those FD&C colors named by numbers) and other synthetic additives can be good for you. Feingold proponents claim that in some instances the regimen can minimize symptoms of ADHD.

Schulson took a closer look at the foods Davin ate. He was shocked to learn just how many kids' staples — even kids' toothpastes — contain dyes like Yellow No. 5 and Blue No. 1. "Eggo waffles, Kraft macaroni and cheese," the chef rattled off. "Even juice boxes and Lunchables," two of Davin's school-meal favorites.

"We don't even realize" how many foods contain artificial ingredients, said the chef. Other Feingold no-no's: the man-made preservatives BHT, BHA and TBHQ. The chef also decided to place strict limits on foods with refined flour or sugar, and cut out high-fructose corn syrup.

It wasn't long before Schulson and his girlfriend, Nina Tinari, were emptying out their Rittenhouse Square condo's cabinets and fridge and going shopping at Whole Foods. There, they realized, artificial-ingredient-less mac and cheese was much, much pricier than Kraft's version. "The mac and cheese that has the dye is 99 cents," said Tinari. "The mac and cheese that doesn't is $3.99."

Still, it was worth it.

"After a week — literally, a week!" of eating differently, Schulson said, Davin's behavior was "like night and day."

He could stay still. He could focus. He came home from school with all "green" and "yellow" lights.

Davin didn't become symptom-free. He still needs to be reminded to pay attention and still makes regular visits to his pediatrician at CHOP's ADHD Center, where his diet is supervised, and where he and his family learn behavior-based interventions. But his symptoms are much more manageable.

RECIPES FOR SUCCESS

Aside from cost, Davin's diet is no sweat. Schulson said there are three simple tricks to getting his kids to stay on the plan.

First, he takes the boys grocery shopping, where they learn about ingredients. When Davin or Jordan picks out something on the "no" list, their dad tells them, "This has X, Y or Z in it. I'm not going to put that in my body. Do you still want to put it in yours?"

Next, he lets them make what they eat. Even little Jordan can slice, squeeze and sauté with his dad's help. Davin, who described himself as the "better chef" of the two brothers (a claim his younger brother proudly disputed), likes to open the refrigerator and ask, "What can we make?"

Last, Schulson keeps Feingold-friendly substitutes on hand. "If I'm gonna take something away, I have to have something else for them." So when their building's doorman gives the kids lollipops, dad trades them for naturally flavored and colored gum balls from their pantry.

Schulson also doesn't deprive Davin of desserts. The youngster loves homemade frozen pops and is allowed chocolate on weekends. Recently, at a birthday party, Davin took it upon himself to scrape the colored icing off his slice of cake.

"I don't want my son to be afraid of food," Schulson said.

Mostly, though, the chef-dad believes that cooking itself makes his boys proud to eat their meals. Said Schulson, "Any time a kid makes something himself, he automatically likes it better".

Many parents, like chef Schulson, are becoming more engaged with their children to win the battle against behavioral challenges through positive changes in nutrition. Do not wait for behavioral symptoms to surface…actively plan nutritional meals with your children. Let them be part of the solution.

Another risk factor consideration when assessing a child or young adult with behavioral symptoms is **reactive HYPOglycemia.** The symptoms of reactive hypoglycemia are very similar to ADHD, including uncontrolled hyperactivity, focus deficiency and fidgeting. Hypoglycemia is a condition that can develop in a young child and go undetected for years masking itself as a behavioral condition. The causes of this physiological condition involve:

- consumption of too much sugar or chemically flavored food in the morning
- not eating enough protein
- not eating enough multiple small meals throughout the day.

Reactive hypoglycemia may be caused by the sugar addiction perpetual cycle as described in Diagram A. This perpetual cycle can begin early in a child's developmental years or later in the teen adolescence years. The onset of this dysfunctional hormonal condition may become rapid and without notice. As a child becomes behaviorally conditioned to consume excessive amounts of sugar containing foods and chemically processed liquids including soda and various "naturally flavored juices", the body begins to develop an addiction.

The addiction to sugar and chemically flavored foods over a period of time triggers the increased release of the hormone dopamine, which is the feel good hormone. As a response to bring the body back to normal, insulin is released by the pancreas to reduce the spiked levels of glucose in the blood. The rapid release of insulin by the pancreas to reduce the rapid increase in blood sugar may create a condition of hypoglycemia wherein the blood sugar falls below the normal range due to too much insulin release.

If the blood sugar becomes too low due to the effects of insulin, then the body develops a **reactive HYPOglycemia** response. This response is critical because the brain will starve without adequate glucose in the blood. The reactive hypoglycemia response by the body to save the brain involves a rapid release of adrenaline (epinephrine) released by the adrenal glands to bring the blood glucose levels back to normal range. Additionally, the body produces adrenaline (epinephrine) from the breakdown of the neurotransmitters, noradrenaline and dopamine as shown in Diagram C. Norepinephrine and dopamine are neurotransmitters critical for cognitive and focused attention. If the body is under constant stress requiring adrenaline (epinephrine) from the breakdown of norepinephrine from dopamine then these neurotransmitters become depleted and may contribute to the onset of ADHD, autism, depression and addictive behaviors. This adrenaline rush into the blood stream has the same symptoms as ADHD. Adrenaline is the body's fight or flight hormone.

- You cannot discipline adrenaline
- You cannot tell adrenaline to be silent
- You cannot tell adrenaline to sit still
- You cannot reason with adrenaline

Excessive and accumulating adrenaline release into the blood stream can create a constant state of stress to the body, and is counterproductive to positive behavioral development. The negative health consequence involves psychological as well as physical factors including sleep disturbances, cardiovascular and inflammation of organ systems. Although the adrenaline response for fight or flight is important, accumulation of this stress hormone needs to be regulated. This regulation is achieved through a whole foods sugar free diet, exercise and effective toxin elimination.

A valuable bio-chemistry lesson for students, parents as well as educators to better understand why behavioral symptoms may develop involves a clear understanding of the hormones adrenaline, noradrenaline and dopamine as well as their production effects in the human body.

CHEMICAL STRUCTURE OF ADRENALINE AND NORADRENALINE

Adrenaline and Noradrenaline are very similar in chemical structure.

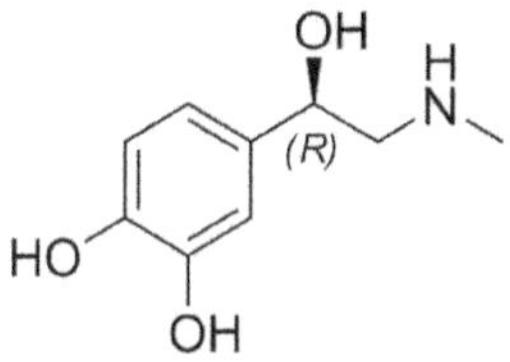

	R = H	Noradrenaline(Norepinephrine)
	R = CH3	Adrenaline(Epinephrine)

L-adrenaline has important biological functions. On the one hand, it belongs, like the chemically related noradrenaline, to the family of adrenal medulla hormones. The hormone has a big influence on the storage and mobilization of glycogen and fatty acids as well as corresponding metabolic pathways in the body. On the other hand, adrenaline is a neurotransmitter of the adrenergic nervous system.

CHEMICAL STRUCTURE OF DOPAMINE

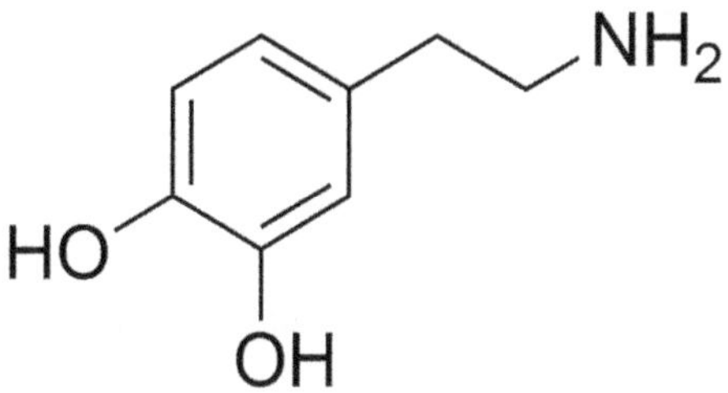

CATECHOLAMINE

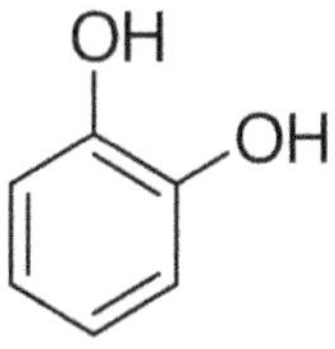

Catecholamine is an monoamine organic compound with a definable benzene and two hydroxyl (OH) side groups as depicted in the above picture. The greatest concentration of catecholamines in the human body are dopamine, norepinephrine and adrenalin (epinephrine). They are water soluble and 50 percent bound to plasma protein. Notice the almost identical chemical structures of these three catecholamines. However, preservation of dopamine and norepinephrine production is critical to behavioral development.

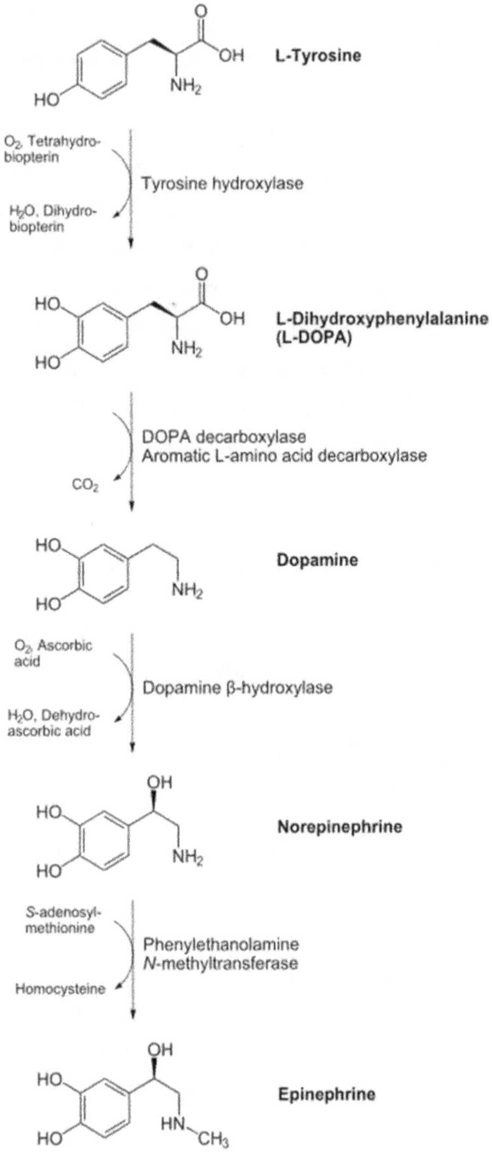

L-Tyrosine

O_2, Tetrahydro-
biopterin

Tyrosine hydroxylase

H_2O, Dihydro-
biopterin

L-Dihydroxyphenylalanine
(L-DOPA)

DOPA decarboxylase
Aromatic L-amino acid decarboxylase

CO_2

Dopamine

O_2, Ascorbic
acid

Dopamine β-hydroxylase

H_2O, Dehydro-
ascorbic acid

Norepinephrine

S-adenosyl-
methionine

Phenylethanolamine
N-methyltransferase

Homocysteine

Epinephrine

THE PRODUCTION OF ADRENALINE (EPINEPHRINE)

The production of these three critical catecholamines begins with the conversion of tyrosine, an amino acid found plentiful in eggs and nuts. Additionally, tyrosine is converted in the body from phenylalanine. Phenylalanine is a naturally occurring amino acid in the body which must be converted. If too much phenylalanine accumulates in the blood stream due to a genetic metabolic condition called phenylketonuria (PKU), then the production of the neurotransmitters essential for cognitive function is diminished and may affect behavioral development in children.

The important fact to understand in the assessment of behavioral symptoms is the realization that the human body has critical hormonal and metabolic processes which may contribute to the onset of behavioral conditions. All healthcare professionals should take the time and evaluate a child's hormone function and nutritional metabolism. Enzymes found in a whole foods diet as well as enzymatic nutritional supplementation are necessary to produce neurotransmitters. The need to prescribe powerful ADHD stimulants and psychiatric medications in young children will be reduced, if these assessments are completed.

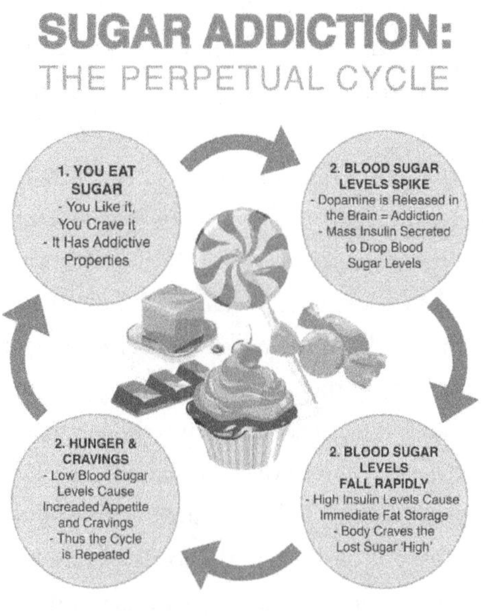

SUGAR ADDICTION:
THE PERPETUAL CYCLE

1. YOU EAT SUGAR
- You Like it, You Crave it
- It Has Addictive Properties

2. BLOOD SUGAR LEVELS SPIKE
- Dopamine is Released in the Brain = Addiction
- Mass Insulin Secreted to Drop Blood Sugar Levels

2. HUNGER & CRAVINGS
- Low Blood Sugar Levels Cause Increased Appetite and Cravings
- Thus the Cycle is Repeated

2. BLOOD SUGAR LEVELS FALL RAPIDLY
- High Insulin Levels Cause Immediate Fat Storage
- Body Craves the Lost Sugar 'High'

DIAGRAM A

The science behind causation of ADHD, autism, depression, and addictive behavioral symptoms in our youth should involve a comprehensive evaluation of adrenalin as well as the sugar addiction cycle. Many cases of ADHD, depression and anxiety in children may be the direct result of this addictive cycle. Become persistent in finding the medical cause of symptoms prior to immediate drug therapy.

In reference to the psychiatric drug-manufacturing industry, Dr. Fred Baughman, neurologist, testified before Congress and stated, "They made a list of the most common symptoms of emotional discomfiture of children; those which bother teachers and parents most, and in a stroke that could not be more devoid of science or Hippocratic motive—termed them a 'disease.' Twenty five years of research, not deserving of the term 'research,' has failed to validate ADHD as a disease. Tragically—the epidemic having grown from 500 thousand in 1985 to over seven million today—this remains the state of the 'science' of ADHD".[19]

Other nutritional considerations regarding causation of ADHD, autism and psychological symptoms in children involve inhibition of nutrient absorption or mal-absorption. Without good nutrition, including a whole-foods diet, enzyme compounds essential for producing neurotransmitters are not adequately manufactured in the body. Therefore, parents should strive to keep their pantries and refrigerators clear of chemically processed food sources.

In conjunction with nutritional factors, physicians, educators, and parents should understand the physiological factors affecting child behavioral development related to the ADHD, autism and psychological symptoms. In doing so, more effective alternative assessment and treatment plans in children may be implemented with far less side effects and deaths, rather than traditional drug therapy as the primary treatment.

Pathophysiology is the science involving the biochemical and physical presentation of a disease or condition. This science correlates the underlying abnormalities and physiologic disturbances. Pathophysiology does not directly address treatment of disease. The focus of this science explains the processes within the human body that cause the symptoms of the condition. ADHD, autism and psychological symptoms are unfortunately treated primarily with drug therapy intervention, which in many cases is associated with long-term harmful side effects to our youth.

The premature use of drug therapy in children is fully endorsed by the current diagnostic guideline from the American Psychiatric Association. This guideline called Diagnostic and Statistical Manual (DSM) of Mental Disorders must be reformed to mandate differential diagnosis and alternative treatment plans before drug therapy is considered. Additionally, prudent drug-monitoring protocols regarding ADHD stimulant and psychiatric drug therapy in children must be reformed.

Effective assessment and treatment plans require a clear knowledge of the pathophysiology of ADHD, autism and psychological symptoms. A differential diagnosis is critical in ADHD and psychiatric conditions. Differential diagnosing determines all possible causes of the behavioral condition, including nutritional, physiological, and environmental as well as psychological risk factors, prior to prematurely treating a child with stimulant or psychiatric medications.

Prior to implementation of alternative treatment plans, physicians, educators, and parents should understand brain pathophysiology as it relates to causation of ADHD and psychiatric symptoms. Symptoms of these conditions can be explained by the maturation process of the prefrontal cortex of the brain. The prefrontal cortex is located in the anterior frontal lobe portion of the brain directly behind the forehead. The primary role of this region is to regulate cognitive function and appropriate behavioral responses or actions.

There are numerous studies involving the science of Response Inhibition (RI), which relates to children and adolescents irrationally acting or responding to various social situations. As a parent of many teenagers, I ask myself everyday why they act the way they do. Magnetic Resonance Imaging (MRI), Single Photon Emission Computed Tomography (SPECT), and Diffusion Tensor Imaging (DTI) brain scanning confirms that the maturation of the prefrontal cortex is not complete until a child reaches their mid-twenties. These studies have also revealed that children have less mature myelin (white matter) in this region than adults. Additionally, children with ADHD had lower levels of dopamine transporters in the brain's reward center than control subjects. These proteins are involved in motivation systems, and the lower levels may explain some of the common symptoms of ADHD such as reduced motivation and inattention.[20]

Why is this important in the cause of ADHD, autism and psychological symptoms? If the maturation process in the prefrontal cortex is slow or deficient due to an incomplete differential diagnosis, then the following occurs. The flow of information between the two frontal lobe hemispheres is compromised. This is explained by the lack of developed white matter in the corpus callosum nerve bundle, which biochemically connects the two hemispheres.

Fetal brain pathophysiology is fast becoming a research hotspot to uncover the cause of autism as well as ADHD. Over 30 percent of all autism cases in the United States have a co-occurrence of ADHD symptoms. Research concludes that ADHD and autism involve similar neurological neurotransmitter pathway dysfunction. Both conditions have similar onset of symptoms due to the inability of removing excessive toxins in the body, primarily from the stomach and intestines. When toxins are not effectively eliminated by the body they can accumulate and cause significant immune dysfunction ultimately leading to significant behavioral challenges. The good news is that ADHD and autism symptoms can be reversed by effectively eliminating risk factors.

Autism Spectrum Disorder (ASD) afflicts approximately 1 in 88 children and is a primary contributor to America's behavioral health crisis. The cumulative autism and ADHD diagnosis in young children presents difficult challenges for millions of families across the United States.

In an effort to uncover the cause of autism, researchers at the University of California-Davis Mind Institute never gave up contention that many cases are the result of an immune disorder. They released their findings in July 2013 via the **Brain & Behavior Research Foundation** and *Translational Psychiatry* ..... stating approximately 25 percent of autism cases may be linked to specific maternal antibodies that cross the placenta during pregnancy, attacking fetal protein brain development with 99 percent predictability.

Researchers identified seven target protein or antigen sites that the mother's auto-antibodies bind. They include cypin, lactase dehydrogenase A & B, STIP1, CRMP1, CRMP2, and Y-box-binding protein. The effect of the mother's auto-antibodies and these antigen sites may create a biomarker of cellular death. Cypin, for example, is one protein that is important in linking neuron cells in the hippocampus, the learning and memory center of the brain, to connect with other neuron cells.

Furthermore, the research group revealed that auto-antibodies injected into eight pregnant female rhesus monkeys created autism like symptoms within the first two years of the young monkey's lives. Although this is encouraging research which explains the cause of a significant number of autism cases, further animal testing is needed prior to developing a human diagnostic test in females to identify the autism inducing auto-antibodies.

The lead researcher in this study holds the auto-antibody patent and is a consultant for Pediatric Bioscience, the company that licensed the technology for development of a diagnostic test within 18 months to detect auto-antibodies in females. This research also encourages development of new therapies to block specific auto-antibody targets which may lower the incidence of autism at birth due to maternal auto-antibodies at the time of conception.

Since approximately 30 percent of all autism cases have a co-occurrence of ADHD symptoms, this new research should also explain ADHD causation. As a pharmacist with over 25 years specializing in ADHD stimulant and psychiatric medications, there is a pharmacological link between Autism Spectrum Disorder and ADHD. Drug therapy used to alleviate, not cure, autism and ADHD symptoms in many cases are similar.

The research findings from the University of California-Davis Mind Institute is groundbreaking, however the important question is......Why are pregnant women producing antibodies that turn rogue and attack fetal proteins critical in neurological development? Is there an environmental, nutritional or neurophysiological explanation that is genetically encoding a mother's immunity to become toxic to her unborn child? Why is autism and ADHD a mysterious epidemic only in America?

Eliminating nutritional and environmental risk factors are critical when considering pregnancy. An expecting mother requires a whole foods diet free from toxins. Toxins are more abundant in today's food supply, including Genetically Modified Organism (GMO) crops proliferating the American landscape.

GMO crops contain bacterial genes which allow survival after herbicide spraying. The bacterial genes also produce Bacillus thuringiensis(Bt), an insect poison. If GMO insect poisons, along with other environmental toxins accumulate in the expectant mother's blood, then an auto-immune response by the fetus may explain why pregnant women develop harmful auto-antibodies causing autism.

Another consideration against GMO food consumption involves the extremely toxic herbicide, glyphosate. Glyphosate is the same chemical in the weed killer Roundup and is one of the most common herbicides used in GMO crop production. In a very short period of time, glyphosate can destroy the body's immunity and the ability to eliminate harmful toxins by the liver.

The negative affect in childhood behavioral development can become significant. Neurotransmitter production may become diminished due to bacterial and yeast overgrowth in the stomach and small intestine. This result occurs because the amino acids required for enzymatic conversion to critical neurotransmitters become adversely affected by the toxic chemical glyphosate. The amino acids adversely affected by glyphosate include tyrosine, phenylalanine and tryptophan.

Until further research validates GMO foods safe for human consumption, expectant mothers should refrain from GMO foods. The Institute for Responsible Technology recommends foods from the www. nonGMOShoppingGuide.com. Additionally, the Coalition Against Overmedicating Our Youth (CAOOY) recommends enzymatic nutritional supplementation which can be found at www.CAOOY.org and linked to www.ProJobaKids.com

With respect to physiological factors, medical research has determined that the onset of ADHD, autism and psychological symptoms may have single or multiple factors contributing to causation. Depletion of neurotransmitters including dopamine, serotonin, and norepinephrine is possible with the onset of behavioral symptoms. Physiological depletion of these neurotransmitters due to mild or significant brain trauma or toxin overload may precipitate the onset of symptoms.

Many clinically diagnosed cases of ADHD and autism fueling the epidemic are actually due to dysfunctional toxin elimination and immunity. There is tremendous scientific debate whether the measles, mumps and rubella (MMR) vaccine given, all at once, to children before the age of two may cause an irreversible toxin overload to a young body. Toxin overload received by a young child can be caused by many factors. If a child's body at age two has a compromised immune system, this vaccine may be too much of an overload for the body to handle. The MMR vaccine should be given in separate doses over a period of three months to protect children from possible toxic overload.

A child's immune system is still developing at age two. Biochemical, hormonal and neurological development is not matured. Digestive elimination of toxins is not developed. So, why is the United States of America vaccinating two year old children with three vaccines at one time? The Centers of Disease Control should mandate a new protective protocol for the administration of the MMR vaccine by dividing the vaccine into three separate injections over three months.

If you suspect your child has immediate onset of behavioral symptoms, contact your pediatrician and be referred to a specialist who has success reversing ADHD and autism conditions. Many cases of successful reversal of ADHD and autism involve the following intervention:

- Detox with enzyme supplementation including glutathione www.ProJobaKids.com
- Remove sugar, dairy, yeast, bread, eggs and wheat gluten from the diet
- Take vitamin D3, magnesium, b-complex, and omega-3 supplementation
- Take an amino acid supplement containing cysteine, glycine and glutamine

On the other hand, trauma or concussive injury to the head may trigger these behavioral conditions immediately, or during a course of years. In many case studies across the United States, osteopathic and chiropractic care is mitigating or reversing trauma injury by decreasing inflammation to the brainstem and spinal cord. Parents faced with the decision to medicate their child should consider a thorough evaluation by a highly qualified chiropractic or osteopathic physician as well as a neurologist to rule out physiological causation to the behavioral condition.

One particular ADHD peer-review case study from the Journal of Manipulative and Physiological Therapeutics (JMPT) involved a five-year-old boy who was helped with chiropractic care after being diagnosed with ADHD at the age of two. The pediatrician prescribed Ritalin, Adderall, and Haldol up until the age of five with no clinical improvement of symptoms. At age five, the child received chiropractic care. During the recording of the child's history, the mother noted a complication at birth. Her child remained in the hospital an extra four days beyond the normal stay. The chiropractic examination and X-rays showed noticeable spinal distortion including a reversal of the normal neck curve indicative of subluxation. Subluxation involves impingement of nerve roots due to dislocation of one or more vertebrae.

In this five-year-old patient, chiropractic care was initiated while monitoring progress. According to the mother, her five-year-old child exhibited positive behavioral changes after the twelfth chiropractic visit. By the twenty-seventh visit, the five-year-old patient experienced considerable improvement. The child was brought to the pediatrician for a follow-up ADHD visit. Upon examination and reassessment of the behavioral condition, the physician determined that a gradual reduction and discontinuance of his medication was appropriate.[21] Review diagram B

This case study from the Journal of Manipulative and Physiological Therapeutics informs parents, educators, and physicians that chiropractic care in conjunction with traditional medicine offers consideration in determining cause of symptoms in children with behavioral conditions. Drug therapy should not be considered until all factors of causation have

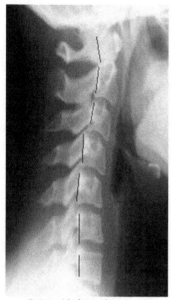 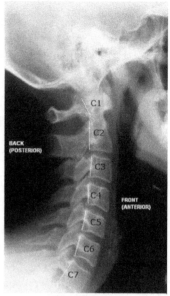

Patient with abnormal X-ray   Normal X-ray and no
and ADHD symptoms.   ADHD symptoms.

DIAGRAM B

been ruled out. Would you as a physician, educator, or parent allow a child to be labeled with an ADHD or psychiatric "disease" and ignore treatment of a physiological condition?

Physicians, educators, parents, and policymakers should unite and reform the current DSM guidelines and implement the Action Plan for Childhood Behavioral Conditions. This new proactive assessment protocol will serve to protect children by mandating an independent differential diagnosis prior to medicating children.

Environmental factors in behavioral development must also be considered prior to medicating children with ADHD or psychiatric conditions. Environmental factors comprise two forms, physical and emotional. The physical environmental factors include toxins in the food, water and air supply. Arsenic is prevalent in many well systems across the country and contributes to heavy metal toxicity in the body, which may lead to causation or etiology in the ADHD or psychiatric behavioral condition. Colloidal silver treatments and an ozonated or reverse osmosis water purification system removes heavy metal toxins from the water supply.

Air quality inside the home is just as important as the air quality outside the home. Carbon monoxide and radon gas must be annually checked for normal limits inside the child's home environment. After living in our home for over ten years, the radon gas level was three times the EPA limit of 4 pCi/liter of air. Radon gas is a naturally occurring by-product of the radioactive decay of uranium in the soil. Radon gas is very common in certain landscapes of the United States. The EPA recommends parents take corrective mitigating action at radon levels above 4 pCi/liter of air within the home.

Once inhaled, radon gas does not travel far into the human body. However, long-term exposure at high concentrations will alter the genome of lung tissue. The alpha radiation particles created from the decay of radon causes mutation within the cellular nucleus of lung tissue.[22] Development of unexplained lung cancer later in life is the primary health concern if children are exposed to radon gas at high levels for an extended period of time. Additionally, chronic long- term exposure will affect other organ systems including those involved in immune function due to deficient cellular oxygenation or oxidative death. As a child develops from birth, healthy air supply must become a critical assessment in childhood behavioral development. Detector kits for carbon monoxide and radon gas are readily available to the public.

A child's emotional environment is extremely important in behavioral development. Positive spiritual or emotional thoughts within a child's mind are very important in the assessment of childhood behavioral development. Children without a positive spiritual and emotional thought process are very susceptible to negative behavioral thinking over time. So how does a parent or educator help guide a child to positive thinking through emotions? Techniques that strengthen a child's emotional mind can be very effective to help alleviate symptoms of the ADHD or psychiatric condition. Parents have a tremendous opportunity to guide their child toward positive emotional development.

First and foremost, parents should indiscriminately act as a filter for their child's friends. Early on in a child's behavioral development, their value system is influenced by relatives, teachers, coaches, as well as their religious faith. Parents have the arduous job of blocking friends that negatively affect a child's character while allowing the association of those who exhibit a positive influence in character. This development of positive character by a child can be achieved by creating a kid-friendly home. A child, throughout all ages of behavioral development, should feel comfortable welcoming all friends into their home. In doing so, a parent has the ability to effectively monitor their child and, more importantly, teenage relationships with friends.

During my experience raising six children, peer pressure may become influential at the early age of eight. Therefore, the earlier a parent invests time to help strengthen a child's self-confidence and emotional thought process, success in the battle against peer pressure will be won. Needless to say, my wife and I as parents like to win. However, the peer pressure challenges brought before us throughout the years were sometimes formidable.

Teamwork and constant communication with our children always got us through the sometimes difficult time of raising teenagers. With five daughters, drama was always a flavor of the week. Looking back now, I would not trade the life-learning experiences for anything in the world. Additionally, increasing self-esteem and self-confidence through visualization, guided imagery, as well as meditation help a child realize their positive emotional potential. These are very specialized techniques that highly qualified professional therapists use to help a child strengthen their subconscious mind influencing the emotive thought process.

Emotions can shape or inhibit thinking. Emotions have projective power over thoughts. Located primarily in the limbic system of the brain, a child's emotions act as filters to form desires and rule immediate thoughts. Emotions provide the framework for the thinking that is to follow. The influence of positive emotional thinking promotes intellectual and respectful character. Children, especially teenagers, must recognize their immediate emotional response. The brain is wired to feed immediate emotional responses to environmental stimuli. Children need to recognize this initial emotion-based response. They have to be aware of their thoughts and their origin. This emotional management process allows a child to act in a way that will lead to the most productive thinking. This means putting the breaks on a child's immediate behavioral response to consider alternative responses.[23]

The causation of childhood behavioral conditions requires the consideration of many factors. Nutritional, physiological, and environmental risk factors should be ruled out prior to implementation of drug therapy. During the past forty years, the process of determining causation of behavioral challenges has been ignored. This ignorance toward the determination of causation has created America's Childhood Behavioral Health Crisis involving Attention Deficit Hyperactivity Disorder, autism, depression as well as addictive behaviors in the child and young adult population.

THE CAUSE OF BEHAVIORAL CHALLENGES
IN CHILDREN CAN BE PUZZLING
Learn the 3 risk factors prior to premature medication therapy

Notes

_____

_____

_____

_____

_____

_____

_____

_____

_____

_____

_____

_____

_____

_____

_____

_____

_____

_____

_____

_____

_____

_____

CHAPTER 4

Attention Deficit Hyperactivity Disorder: America's Epidemic

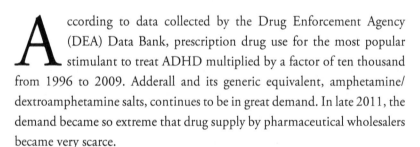

According to data collected by the Drug Enforcement Agency (DEA) Data Bank, prescription drug use for the most popular stimulant to treat ADHD multiplied by a factor of ten thousand from 1996 to 2009. Adderall and its generic equivalent, amphetamine/dextroamphetamine salts, continues to be in great demand. In late 2011, the demand became so extreme that drug supply by pharmaceutical wholesalers became very scarce.

The American Academy of Pediatrics states that 9 percent of the children in the United States, age five to seventeen, account for over five million patients taking stimulant drug therapy to treat ADHD and increases to over twelve million patients including late teens and young adults consuming stimulant or psychiatric medications. This trend is alarming and poses a direct threat to the health and security of our next generation, since long-term stimulant drug therapy increases development of other high-risk behavioral conditions.

America's children consume over three times the ADHD stimulant and psychiatric drugs compared to the world's children combined. This statistic, according to data obtained by *Scientific American*, along with the fact that the DEA has prosecuted many cases in the young adult population abusing and diverting these drugs, represents America's ADHD epidemic, which directly contributes to the Behavioral Health Crisis in America.

Safety considerations regarding long-term use of ADHD stimulant drug therapy requires reexamination in children due to increases in health risk. According to the Substance Abuse and Mental Health Services Administration, over 23,000 teen and young adults were rushed to hospital emergency rooms in 2012. This statistic represents a 400 percent increase since 2005. More alarming is the fact that over 30 percent of these emergencies involved the consumption of alcohol with powerful amphetamine stimulants. Consumption of ADHD stimulant amphetamine medications when combined with excessive alcohol may lead to anxiety, minor depression, major depression, psychosis and death. Furthermore, the National Institute of Health warns families that over 30 percent of college students are taking powerful ADHD stimulant amphetamines, most commonly Adderall, illegally without a documented prescription.

Adderall is the most abused controlled substance Class II narcotic on college campuses in the United States. Pharmaceutical sales of all stimulants eclipsed nine billion dollars in 2012 compared to approximately four billion dollars in 2007. In my 25 years of pharmacy practice, the time has come for "a call to action", and help society understand the long term dangers of prescribing stimulant amphetamines as well as psychiatric medications in young children.

In a recent survey, only 1 in 100 parents were aware that their child was taking ADHD stimulant amphetamines like the Adderall study drug while at college. Suicide is now the second leading cause of death in the United States college student population. The solution to the Adderall epidemic involves a comprehensive assessment of nutritional, physiological and environmental risk factors prior to premature drug therapy, especially in young children.

Before an understanding of "why" Adderall has become the most abused and diverted controlled substance for cognitive study on college campuses in the United States, we should realize the impact that the recent prescribing history of stimulant amphetamines in children has created.

The misuse and overprescribing of ADHD stimulant amphetamine and psychiatric medications in the child foster care system was uncovered by the largest drug audit in American history....the Government Accountability Office drug audit of 2008 through 2010. The alarming results were revealed to the public in December 2011. The results are a contributing factor in America's ADHD epidemic. ADHD stimulant amphetamines may be very effective in the short term by increasing cognitive function and decreasing hyperactivity. However, the long term effects are now evident, especially when children as young as the age of three begin therapy. The potential increased risk for anxiety, minor depression, major depression, psychosis and ultimately suicide is now warned by the FDA.

Many United States senators, including Charles Schumer from New York, are researching legislation requiring more strict protocols prior to college students gaining access to powerful stimulants. California State University at Fresno has already implemented a very strict program for college students seeking stimulant study drugs, like Adderall.

Since the new program began, there has been a dramatic decline of students making doctor appointments for stimulant therapy at their university health centers. Students claim there is too much red tape in obtaining stimulant drugs like Adderall, since mandatory mental health assessments are required as well as psychotherapy requirements for future refills of the medication.

The solution for the ADHD epidemic involves a new vision of assessing and treating children as discussed in the Action Plan for Childhood Behavioral Conditions. This new vision of assessment is already in practice within many institutions across America. Additionally, the National Institute of Mental Health in Washington DC states that the assessment system in place for the last 40 years "lacks validity, and patients with mental disorders deserve better".

The new vision assessment process as described in The Action Plan for Childhood Behavioral conditions, created by the non-profit Coalition Against Overmedicating Our Youth (CAOOY).....involves ruling out nutritional, physiological and environmental risk factors prior to premature drug therapy, especially in young children.

Cardiovascular adverse drug reactions associated with stimulant therapy is escalating in the teenage and young adult population. The long-term effects of ADHD stimulant medications are now known and may adversely affect childhood behavioral development according to the six-year Johns Hopkins Child Center Study.

ADHD Symptoms Persist for Most Young Children Despite Treatment
THE JOHNS HOPKINS CHILD CENTER STUDY
February 11, 2013
-Results spell need for more effective therapies, earlier intervention

Nine out of 10 young children with moderate to severe attention-deficit hyperactivity disorder (ADHD) continue to experience serious, often severe symptoms and impairment long after their original diagnoses and, in many cases, despite treatment, according to a federally funded multi-center study led by investigators at the Johns Hopkins Children's Center.

The study, published online Feb. 11, 2013 in the Journal of the American Academy of Child & Adolescent Psychiatry, is the largest long-term analysis to date of preschoolers with ADHD, the investigators say, and sheds much-needed light on the natural course of a condition that is being diagnosed at an increasingly earlier age.

"ADHD is becoming a more common diagnosis in early childhood, so understanding how the disorder progresses in this age group is critical," says lead investigator Mark Riddle, M.D., a pediatric psychiatrist at the Johns Hopkins Children's Center. "We found that ADHD in preschoolers is a chronic and rather persistent condition, one that requires better long-term behavioral treatments than we currently have."

The study shows that nearly 90 percent of the 186 youngsters followed continued to struggle with ADHD symptoms six years after diagnosis. Children taking ADHD medication had just as severe symptoms as those who were medication-free, the study found.

Children with ADHD, ages 3 to 5, were enrolled in the study, treated for several months, after which they were referred to community pediatricians for ongoing care. Over the next six years, the researchers used detailed reports from parents and teachers to track the children's behavior, school performance and the frequency and severity of three of ADHD's hallmark symptoms: inattention, hyperactivity and impulsivity. The children also had full diagnostic workups by the study's clinicians at the beginning, halfway through and at the end of the research.

Symptom severity scores did not differ significantly between the more than two-thirds of children on medication and those off medication, the study showed. Specifically, 62 percent of children taking anti-ADHD drugs had clinically significant hyperactivity and impulsivity, compared with 58 percent of those not taking medicines.

And 65 percent of children on medication had clinically significant inattention, compared with 62 percent of their medication-free counterparts. The investigators caution that it remains unclear whether the lack of medication effectiveness was due to suboptimal drug choice or dosage, poor adherence, medication ineffectiveness per se or some other reason.

"Our study was not designed to answer these questions, but whatever the reason may be, it is worrisome that children with ADHD, even when treated with medication, continue to experience symptoms, and what we need to find out is why that is and how we can do better," Riddle says.

Children who had oppositional defiant disorder or conduct disorder in addition to ADHD were 30 percent more likely to experience persistent ADHD symptoms six years after diagnosis, compared with children whose sole diagnosis was ADHD.

ADHD is considered a neurobehavioral condition and is marked by inability to concentrate, restlessness, hyperactivity and impulsive behavior. It can have profound and long-lasting effects on a child's intellectual and emotional development, Riddle says. It can impair learning, academic performance, peer and family relationships and even physical safety. Past research has found that children with ADHD are at higher risk for injuries and hospitalizations.

More than 7 percent of U.S. children are currently treated for ADHD, the investigators say. The annual economic burden of the condition is estimated to be between $36 billion and $52 billion, according to researchers.

Other Johns Hopkins investigators involved in the research included Elizabeth Kastelic, M.D., and Gayane Yenokyan, Ph.D.

The other institutions involved in the research were Columbia University Medical Center, Duke University, the Nathan Kline Institute, University of California-Irvine and University of California-Los Angeles.

The research was funded by the National Institute of Mental Health under grant numbers: U01 MH60642 (Johns Hopkins), U01MH60848 (Duke University Medical Center), U01MH60943 (New York University Child Study Center), U01MH60903 (Columbia University), U01 MH60833 (University of California-Irvine) and U01H60900 (University of California-Los Angeles).

Many researchers across America have expressed warnings regarding a lack of normal development of the brain with long-term use of stimulant drug therapy. Furthermore, stimulant therapy may exacerbate symptoms of underlying depression, anxiety, and aggression due to underlying medical conditions.

Americans should unite and not ask whether children are being overmedicated. The question today should be… Why are children in America overmedicated? What are the long-term health consequences? And, what is the solution to reverse this alarming trend in America?

Although many children in America exhibit an immediate positive response to stimulant drug therapy for their behavioral ADHD symptoms, the possible long-term side effects must be given further scrutiny. The FDA requires a mandatory Med Guide alert for all ADHD stimulant as well as psychiatric medications due to adverse drug reactions and deaths associated with their use in children. The United States leads the world in overall adverse drug reaction deaths, which includes overmedicating. This statistic is the third leading cause of death in America, after cardiac disease and cancer.

In order to reverse this alarming trend, parents as well as guardians of children identified with ADHD symptoms should understand possible risk factor causes of symptoms. ADHD is a condition, not a mental health disease as stated in the Diagnostic and Statistical Manual of Mental Disorders published by the American Psychiatric Association. I strongly urge citizens in America to contact their representatives in Washington, DC, to legislate reform regarding the recently released edition of the DSM 2013 publication and remove ADHD as a mental health illness. Attention Deficit Disorder has three distinct clinical presentations:

1. **Inattentive ADD** presents predominately in the adolescent female population. Symptoms of condition include daydreaming, confusion, slower movement, disengaged, forgetful, and distracted and lack of focus.
2. **Impulsive ADD** manifests in children through impatience, vulgar or inappropriate speech, and chronic interruption in conversation with others.
3. **Hyperactive ADD or ADHD** is the most common presentation of the ADD behavioral condition and occurs predominately in adolescent males. This condition is also called attention deficit hyperactivity disorder and is diagnosed twice as often in males as in the adolescent female population.

The most prescribed stimulant drug therapies, although very effective in many cases, require prudent monitoring protocols. They include the following:

Amphetamine class:
1. Adderall (tablet)—FDA approved three years and older.
2. Adderall XR (long-acting capsule)—FDA approved three and older
3. Vyvanse (long-acting capsule)—FDA approved three and older

Methylphenidate class:
1. Ritalin (tablet)—FDA approved six years and older
2. Methylin (tablet)—FDA approved six years and older
3. Concerta (long-acting tablet)—FDA approved six years and older
4. Focalin XR (long-acting capsule)—FDA approved six and older

Non-stimulant class:
1. Strattera (atomoxetine) is a non-stimulant antidepressant medication that increases blood levels of the neurotransmitter

norepinephrine. Most commonly used in ADHD patients who exhibit adverse reactions to stimulant therapy.

Long-term stimulant therapy in ADHD children may mask depressive disorders including minor depression/dysthymia or generalized anxiety disorder. Additionally, stimulant drug therapy, in and of itself, may also increase the child's propensity to develop chronic irritability leading to a depressive behavioral condition with long-term usage. Current Med Guide alerts for stimulant therapy in children approved by the FDA include the following:

1. Call your doctor if your child develops new mental symptoms or problems, mainly hearing voices or believing things that are not real.
2. Call your doctor if your child develops new aggressive behavior.
3. Call your doctor if your child develops bipolar depression
4. Stimulant therapy is contraindicated in patients with anxiety disorder, glaucoma, cardiovascular dysfunction, history of drug abuse and motor tics (abnormal movements or sounds).

The long-term side effects of stimulant therapy in children, although not known years ago due to lack of long-term clinical studies, are now more defined. The FDA has mandated Med Guide alerts for stimulant and psychiatric medication therapy in children due to the potential for causing harm. Therefore, physicians and pharmacists need to do more in educating the public regarding long-term side effects of stimulant therapy in children.

Simply stating to a parent that these are all the possible side effects on a Med Guide alert is not adequate. Pharmacists and physicians should inform parents the importance of ruling out nutritional, physiological, and environmental risk factors prior to prematurely medicating children. Furthermore, physicians and pharmacists should realize that a child prematurely medicated with powerful stimulant or psychiatric drug therapy prior to comprehensively ruling out underlying causation to the behavioral condition is a form of overmedicating. This premature medication process could be potentially dangerous to a child's long-term health and behavioral development.

Pharmacists are expert medication advisors (EMA). The national chain pharmacies as well as institutional pharmacies have a great opportunity to positively impact childhood behavioral development. Children prescribed high-risk medications including stimulant and psychiatric medications require a greater degree of medication counseling. A counseling program for child stimulant and psychiatric drug therapy, initiated by national chain pharmacies, will provide the public with increased knowledge regarding the safe and effective use of high-risk drug therapy in children. Currently, these precautions for child safety are being ignored by the national chain pharmacy industry.

For example, a seventeen-year-old patient contacted me regarding her new ADHD stimulant prescription for Vyvanse 50 mg. She was taking this drug for a month and developed chronic headaches. She stated no history of chronic headaches prior to being prescribed Vyvanse. Although headache is a common side effect of amphetamine stimulant drug therapy, I informed her to request a thorough cardiac assessment including an EKG. She contacted me three weeks later stating that the doctor had to lower the dose due to a minor abnormality in the EKG.

At a 30-mg dose, this patient's side effects disappeared while maintaining therapeutic cognitive results. This case stresses the importance to start a new patient with lower stimulant drug therapy to avoid harmful side effects that may lead to cardiovascular disease. Drug therapy should only be initiated after a comprehensive differential diagnosis ruling out all risk factors.

The following is a tragedy that can happen when monitoring protocols are not utilized. Matthew was a fourteen-year-old boy who suddenly died of cardiac arrest due to long-term use of the ADHD stimulant Ritalin (methylphenidate). According to the chief pathologist, Matthew died of small vessel damage caused by the vasoconstrictive effects of methylphenidate. Matthew did not have a preexisting cardiac condition. At the time of autopsy, Matthew's heart weighed approximately 50 grams more than the average adult male heart. The pathologist stated in his autopsy that methylphenidate, the powerful stimulant drug, caused significant vascular damage leading to the sudden death of fourteen-year-old Matthew. His death certificate read: "Death caused from long-term use of methylphenidate".[24]

Matthew's death is not an isolated incident. There are thousands of adverse drug event cases involving ADD stimulant and psychiatric medications every year, many of which do not get reported to the FDA Adverse Drug Reaction system.

How and why did Matthew's tragedy occur? While in first grade, Matthew was evaluated by his school's social worker who believed he had ADHD. The school's social worker warned Matthew's parents that if they did not get him on medication, then the department of protective services could charge neglect for his educational and emotional needs. This particular school social worker stated that ADHD was a "real brain disorder, and a mild medication would stimulate his brain stem to help Matthew focus." Scared and intimidated, Matthew's parents gave in to the school's demands. His first dose of methylphenidate began at age seven.[25]

1. The parents were never told of harmful and possible toxic side effects of the medication.

2. The parents were never told that the DEA classifies methylphenidate as a controlled substance, schedule II class narcotic.

3. The parents were never told that methylphenidate is one of the top ten abused drugs.

4. The parents were never told that ADD is a nonscientific disorder with extremely uncertain validity to causation.

5. The parents were never told alternative treatment plans.

6. The parents were never told that nutritional, physiological, or environmental manifestations could cause symptoms related to the American Psychiatric Association's ADD labeling.

7. The parents were never told that some school districts receive additional money from state and federal governments for children labeled as ADD or psychiatric disorder.

8. The parents were never told that over fifty percent of foster children in the United States are overprescribed these medications paid by the taxpayers through state Medicaid programs lobbied by the psychiatric drug industry.

Most importantly, Matthew's parents were never told what the current ADHD diagnosing guidelines really meant. Because the DSM labeled him with ADHD, he was also labeled as having a mental illness listed in accordance with the DSM-IV for psychiatry. Until recently, the FDA now mandates all pharmacies provide a Med Guide alert for all stimulant and psychiatric medications dispensed to children. Unfortunately, the current med guides do not mandate extensive critical monitoring as well as differential diagnosing protocols in children.

This was Matthew's tragic story. The last seven years of Matthew's life was devoted to a fight involving the toxic side effects of a drug that was not prudently monitored. This story does not stop with Matthew. There are thousands of tragic stories every year involving psychiatric drugs and powerful stimulants prescribed to children and young adults.

The Action Plan for Childhood Behavioral Conditions should be implemented to protect our children from the misuse of psychiatric and stimulant drugs. This step by step action plan recommends physicians consider a root cause analysis or etiology including nutritional, physiological, and environmental risk factors which may cause the child's behavioral symptoms. Most importantly, physicians should consider alternative treatment plans for an extended period of time prior to prescribing stimulant or psychiatric drugs in children. The differential diagnosis protocol should be included in a child's assessment prior to drug therapy.

Our nation's school administrators, teachers, parents, and healthcare professionals will unite and become the leaders of this initiative to help children receive new comprehensive assessment information as well as the behavioral assessments that have been in place for over 40 years. Additionally, this action plan will unite parents, educators, physicians, pharmacists, and policymakers to begin safer diagnosing as well as treatment protocols rather than prematurely medicating our youth. Specifically, the Action Plan for

Childhood Behavioral Conditions will rectify the injustices against our foster and non-foster children during the last fifteen years, as we aggressively move forward to eliminate the ADHD epidemic causing the Behavioral Health Crisis in America.

Notes

_____

_____

_____

_____

_____

_____

_____

_____

_____

_____

_____

_____

_____

_____

_____

_____

_____

_____

_____

_____

_____

CHAPTER 5

Plan of Correction: Pharmacists and Physicians Lead to Protect Children

In an effort to develop a prudent plan of correction for prescribing ADHD stimulant and psychiatric medications to our youth, pharmacists and physicians in community practice as well as institutional practice must communicate and protect children. Currently, this lack of communication has become a contributing factor causing the childhood behavioral health crisis in America. For too long, pharmacists have looked the other way when dispensing powerful stimulant amphetamine and psychiatric drug therapy, outside recommended protocols for children.

Pharmacists and physicians communicate on a regular basis in institutional or hospital practice, through guidelines established by the Centers for Medicaid and Medicare Services (CMS) under supervision of the United States Department of Health and Human Services. This communication mainly occurs through the pharmacy and therapeutics committee of the institution or hospital. CMS should mandate a strict implementation of Cognitive Behavioral Therapy (CBT) as well as differential diagnosing to determine cause of symptoms while a child or young adult is stabilized from a behavioral crisis during hospitalization.

This intervention would allow lower and less frequent dosing of medication while allowing trained therapists to concentrate on strengthening the patient's emotional thought process.

Similar guidelines should be implemented in community practice for safe and effective medication treatment. For example, a psychiatrist in community practice should initiate and refer the child for an independent differential diagnosis. A child's complete history and physical examination should be fully assessed by an independent medical doctor to rule out underlying medical causes to the ADHD or psychiatric condition. Throughout this process, the child should engage in at least two CBT treatment programs prior to ADHD or psychiatric medication. Policymakers in Washington, DC, should engage in productive discussions and mandate reform. The National Institute of Mental Health in Washington DC has already initiated a positive reform for the diagnosing of behavioral conditions.

The National Institute of Mental Health Research Domain Criteria (RDoC) is in the research planning stages and will soon become a very useful tool for the clinical assessment of risk factors causing behavioral illness symptoms. The RDoC serves to transform the diagnosing protocols that have been in place for over 40 years within the dysfunctional Diagnostic and Statistical Manual. Specialties in neuroscience including image technology, genetics as well as cognitive sciences will help determine cause of behavioral symptoms prior to premature drug therapy.

The RDoC should be immediately implemented to guide physicians toward comprehensive bio-assessments prior to premature drug therapy. In doing so, physicians will offer hope for millions of parents trying to help their child with behavioral struggles rule out causative risk factors for ADHD, depression as well as addictive behaviors.

Another solution within the plan of correction to stop the overmedicating-our-youth epidemic involves a more strict oversight by the Department of Health and Human Services in Washington DC to reform the child foster care system with respect to prudent prescribing of ADHD stimulant and psychiatric medications.

This plan of correction involves informed consent for foster care children receiving ADHD or psychiatric drug therapy. The doctrine of "informed consent" in the practice of medicine involves a duty or responsibility by the physician to actively inform the child and parent all aspects of a proposed procedure or therapy. I recommend adherence to general guidelines regarding the form described as the *Informed Consent Document for ADHD and Psychiatric Medications.* This document would mandate that the patient, parent, or legal guardian be informed verbally and in writing as such:

1. Nature of ADHD or psychiatric diagnosis and proposed drug therapy.
2. Purpose of the proposed drug therapy.
3. Risk and benefits of proposed drug therapy.
4. The probability of anticipated risks and benefits of drug therapy.
5. The risks and benefits of not receiving drug therapy.
6. Alternative assessment and treatment plan instead of proposed drug therapy explaining risks and benefits.
7. A signed copy of the Informed Consent Document for ADHD and Psychiatric Medications should be presented to the retail pharmacy with a valid signed prescription by the physician.

The pharmacy would be required to staple this consent form to the back of the new prescription for all stimulant and psychiatric medications in children up to age eighteen.

Alternative assessment and treatment plans prior to drug therapy are gradually being recommended by psychiatrists across America. Many prominent physicians are rising up and leading the charge for the protection of children, giving them a voice they never had before. The United States Secretary of Health and Human Services should take the lead from the psychiatrists who are practicing medicine in this prudent manner. Additionally, the United States Department of Health and Human Services should require all state mental health directors adopt a comprehensive differential diagnosis assessment as well as informed consent initiatives. The implementation of the Informed Consent Document for ADHD and Psychiatric Medications in community retail practice for children will serve to unite all physicians and pharmacists for safe medication therapy intervention only after a comprehensive differential diagnosis has been completed.

Children trapped in temporary foster care should be relocated to a permanent, loving and legally adopted home environment. Policymakers in Washington, DC, should implement incentives for adoption agencies to increase the movement of children out of the foster care system. Over time, the funding for the foster care system should be drastically decreased while improving the function of adoption agencies to help children achieve positive childhood behavioral development through a permanent home environment. The social benefit by dramatically increasing this process would eliminate victimization of children due to excessive overprescribing within the child foster care system, just as waste and abuse runs rampant in the adult Medicare system. Education for appropriate treatment protocols in children should be fully disclosed to foster care as well as non-foster care parents.

The positive impact of increasing the adoption process for children is exemplified by the life of Dave Thomas, founder of the Wendy's restaurant chain. Through a loving adopting family, Dave Thomas was able to initiate great contributions to our society during his lifetime. Currently, the Dave Thomas Foundation for Adoption financially supports organizations including the Congressional Coalition on Adoption Institute (CCAI) that help children permanently move from the foster care system to loving adopted homes. Legislation in Washington must facilitate the proliferation of these coalitions with similar functions and goals to help victimized children achieve positive childhood behavioral development.

Furthermore, national retail pharmacy chains as well as institutional pharmacies should adopt an aggressive campaign to warn the public about the dangers of overmedicating our youth. The retail community pharmacy industry should advertise and recommend the Action Plan for Childhood

Behavioral Conditions. This recommendation should be wide in scope and objectively seek to educate parents, policymakers, school administrators, as well as physicians on a national level.

As expert medication advisors, pharmacists provide critical knowledge as well as the final assessment in prudent use of drug therapy in children. They are leaders of their industry and provide a public information service for parents, educators, and physicians. Physicians and pharmacists should unite and demand reform by their professional governing bodies to implement the safe, effective medication protocols in children. The Action Plan for Childhood Behavioral Conditions is an effective resource for parents, educators, physicians and pharmacists to proceed with safe and effective assessment and treatment plans as well as recommending prudent drug-monitoring protocols. A complete differential diagnosis is critical prior to medicating our youth. Many psychiatrists across America are realizing the importance of reform to protect our children.

Dr. Christopher Bellonci, child psychiatrist and author of the 2010 Tufts study, which showed approximately 50 percent of states either did not have or were still in the process of developing policies regarding foster care psychotropic drug use, thinks the Department of HHS guidance for best practices is not good enough. Dr. Bellonci further related in the GAO report "states need to require pharmacies to document actual psychotropic drugs given foster children. We need to be able to benchmark states around one another, and then at least it is all public record".[26]

Although foster children have a preponderance of emotional and behavioral conditions due to their lack of positive parental guidance within a family unit, many physicians believe that the magnitude of excessive psychotropic drug prescribing is not justified. "The general consensus is that when you are treating young children, you always try behavioral intervention before you go to medication. There are a lot of people, you need to talk and find out as much as you can about what the child's behavior is like in a variety of situations before making a determination that you are going to use something like a very powerful medication to treat them," relates Dr. Charles Zeenah, director of Child and Adolescent Psychiatry at Tulane University.[27]

The Government Accountability Office Child Foster Care drug audit report further discovered that many states are not following accountability guidelines as required by law in accordance with the Fostering Connections to Success and Increasing Adoption Act of 2008 as well as the Child and Family Services Improvement and Innovation Act passed in September 2011. Parents, educators, pharmacists, as well as physicians should unite and understand the new differential diagnosis protocol via the Action Plan for Childhood Behavioral Conditions. Children deserve a voice for prudent assessing, prescribing and monitoring of behavioral symptoms.

Physicians and pharmacists across America appreciate positive commentary by the public, especially when they are making a positive impact in child behavioral development through prudent medical care and appropriate drug-monitoring protocols. Together, physicians and pharmacists provide a critical role in eliminating the victimization of foster and non-foster care children.

Parents, educators, physicians, pharmacists, and policymakers should unite for the common good of childhood behavioral development. Positive behavioral health in children is a much greater societal benefit than the wealth corporations around the world are generating via poor oversight of prescribing habits in child psychiatric care. This fact is finally achieving national attention through the inspiring work at the Coalition Against Overmedicating Our Youth (CAOOY), Congressional Coalition for Adoption Institute (CCAI), Citizens Commission on Human Rights (CCHR) and the United States Government Accountability Office.

On December 1, 2011, the Senate Committee on Homeland Security and Government Affairs held a hearing on the victimization of children in the foster care system due to overmedicating our youth. The Government Accountability Office reported findings to committee chairman, U.S. Senator Thomas Carper. A significant lack of mental health care and overuse of psychiatric medications was the major alarm during the last four years of the Foster Youth Intern Report by the CCAI.

In the United States, there is only one foster care home for every four children in need. This forces the foster care system to house multiple children within one home. The ADHD and psychiatric drugs are implemented as behavioral control mechanisms, according to the GAO report.

Senator Carper in response to the GAO report states "Congress has a responsibility to try to get to the bottom of this, and armed with information, to make sure that oversight is changed, that is going to be beneficial to children." Senator Carper will be a crucial policymaker as a plan of correction takes shape and direction from his committee. He will be instrumental in uniting physicians, the pharmacy retail leaders, as well as Health and Human Services officials in Washington for the purpose of implementing prudent corrective action.

Some experts in the practice of psychiatry are now realizing that the lack of differential diagnosing for bipolar disorder in foster children is out of control and void of oversight. Stephen Crystal, PhD and director of the Center of Education and Research on Mental Health Therapeutics at Rutgers University, states that while foster kids may be three times as likely to be diagnosed with bipolar disorder, "the validity of these diagnoses is uncertain, and the fact of being in foster care may itself increase the likelihood of psychiatric conditions being diagnosed".[28]

State Medicaid spends at least six billion dollars a year, nearly 30 percent of its entire drug budget on psychiatric drugs, which is more than double what was spent in 1999, according to the Centers for Medicaid and Medicare Services.

The Congressional Coalition for Adoption Institute conducts a program of training new foster parents to eliminate overcrowding and provide individual care and eventually move the child to a permanent adopted home environment. In December 2011, an eleven-year-old boy from Texas, named Keonte, testified before Congress with his adopted parents and stated that he did not want any child to be a victim of overmedicating. He testified before Congress and thanked his adopted parents for their love in helping him find a good therapist to sort through the issues of his painful past, a past that consisted of parental neglect and excessive medicating with psychiatric medications.

Keonte was often left home alone with his one-year-old sister and eventually became a ward of the state at age four. He was placed with a relative who repeatedly beat him with belts, switches, and extension cords. His environment caused him emotional scarring as well as physical scarring.

The State of Texas transferred Keonte between six different foster homes over a four-year period. His trauma was treated with inappropriate use of psychiatric medications including Lexapro, Seroquel, Depakote, Vyvanse, and Clonidine. Keonte stated to Congress "I was put on bipolar meds. I am not bipolar at all".[29]

He became very fortunate after his interview with ABC News. Keonte was finally selected for adoption into a secure and loving home. They effectively sought the best psychotherapist for Keonte. After a long process of "talking" about his painful family past and gradual tapering of his medication, Keonte is no longer classified as bipolar or ADHD. Without the adoptive intervention and the differential diagnosis involving psychotherapy, Keonte would still be stigmatized as a ward of the state without hope or vision for a prosperous future. Our society should intervene, even if we have to successfully adopt one foster child at a time. The CCAI is supported by the Dave Thomas Foundation for Adoption as well as the Kellogg Foundation, which benefit underprivileged children within the foster care system.

Another very influential organization protecting our children is the Citizens Commission on Human Rights (CCHR). They are the world's leading mental health watchdog commission creating a free public search engine featuring

1. 160 psychiatric drug warnings from international drug regulatory agencies,
2. 150 drug studies from international medical journals, and
3. over two hundred thousand adverse reaction reports on psychiatric drugs filed with the FDA.

The CCHR is the only organization offering this free service to the public. They are primarily responsible for influencing the enactment of over 150 laws protecting individuals from abusive mental health practices as well as the Child and Family Services Improvement and Innovation Act of September 2011.

The Coalition Against Overmedicating Our Youth (CAOOY) offers free educational and medication consultations while raising public awareness of appropriate use of medications in children around the world. CAOOY is the World Advocate for Children. The CAOOY mission helps parents help their children determine cause of behavioral symptoms by providing free bio-assessment recommendations as well as consultations for safe medication protocols. CAOOY also offers this free consultation service to parents who adopt foster care children with extensive drug regimens requiring guidance in their child's medication therapy. CAOOY coordinates with school districts to offer free consultations as well as bio-assessment recommendations to rule out underlying causation prior to medicating our youth.

CAOOY has formed an alliance with the Regional Anti-drug Education Outreach (www.RADEO.org) as well as ACalltoActions (www. ACalltoActions.com). ACalltoActions was founded by Kimberlee Schultz, national children's storybook author of the popular StarPals and Eugene Irvin, lead field investigator.

A Call to Action is a lifestyle choice with visionary objectives to protect children's rights. They persevere in getting the correct information to the public regarding injustices committed toward children...the CAOOY/ ACalltoActions alliance empowers those within their organizations to become motivated using the highest standards of integrity, accountability and transparency. With vision, action and collaboration, they produce positive results.

The CAOOY/RADEO alliance offers free consultative and educational guidance, helping teens and young adults win the battle against addictive behaviors leading to opiate addiction. RADEO is co-founded by Judge Jodi Debbrecht Switalski and addiction behavior program director, Elizabeth Reader from Milford Counseling Services in Milford, Michigan. Together CAOOY and RADEO provide concrete guidance helping our youth get back on a positive mental health pathway.

With national and international public support for reformation against overmedicating our youth, the CCAI, CCHR, ACalltoActions, RADEO and CAOOY as well as other organizations across America are offering bright light solutions to eliminate overmedicating our youth. At the national level of government, research by the National Institute of Mental Health in Washington DC is providing a positive new vision of diagnosing through the Research Domain Criteria. This new diagnosing criteria in conjunction with The Action Plan for Childhood Behavioral Conditions requires immediate implementation, and will give physicians a better perspective on diagnosing the cause of behavioral symptoms rather than prescribing premature drug therapy in young children, which serves to reform a system that is..........

Over Medicating Our Youth

Notes

_____

_____

_____

_____

_____

_____

_____

_____

_____

_____

_____

_____

_____

_____

_____

_____

_____

_____

_____

_____

_____

Ask the Pharmacist • www.CAOOY.org

Helping Determine Causation of Behavioral Conditions

Donations Provide Free Clinical Bio-Assesment and Medication Consultations

CAOOY

Coalition Against Overmedicating Our Youth

WORLD ADVOCATE FOR CHILDREN©

CHAPTER 6

Solutions for America's Epidemic

Before solutions involving a step by step Action Plan for Childhood Behavioral Conditions can be implemented to reverse the epidemic, Americans must agree that today's children, nationally and internationally, hold the key to the future success of our world in which we live. The positive behavioral growth and development of today's children must be protected and nurtured to prevent negative influences from entering their lives.

Unfortunately, the current Diagnostic and Statistical Manual of Mental Disorders guideline adopted and published by the American Psychiatric Association has not protected our youth for over forty years. Furthermore, thousands of children are dying every year with no voice to reveal their suffering from medications prescribed without proper monitoring protocols and dosing parameters. The deaths and suicides by children due to inconclusive diagnosing and the overprescribing of ADHD stimulant and psychiatric medications often go unreported to the United States Food and Drug Administration.

The Action Plan for Childhood Behavioral Conditions as outlined by the non-profit Coalition Against Overmedicating Our Youth

(CAOOY) should be implemented to protect our children from the misuse of psychiatric and stimulant drug therapy. This action plan recommends that physicians consider a root cause analysis or etiology including nutritional, physiological, or environmental risk factors causing a child's behavioral symptoms. Most importantly, physicians should consider alternative assessment and treatment plans for an extended period of time prior to prescribing powerful stimulant or psychiatric medications.

Parents, educators and all healthcare professionals should understand the clinical fact that childhood ADHD, depression as well as addictive behavior have underlying as well as linked risk factors which may cause symptoms. There exists a direct correlation between mental health and physical health involving the onset of childhood behavioral symptoms. For example, depressive symptoms in school age children have similar clinical signs related to ADHD. These signs include but not limited to:

- fatigue
- hyperactivity
- anxiety, aggression
- drop in school grades
- feeling sad or hopeless
- chronic digestive problems
- low self-esteem.

This action plan will unite parents, educators, physicians, policymakers, and the retail pharmacy industry to begin safe and effective monitoring as well as diagnosing protocols rather than prematurely overmedicating our youth. Specifically, the Action Plan for Childhood Behavioral Conditions will rectify the injustices committed against our foster and non-foster children during the last fifteen years.

INFORMATIONAL GUIDE REFERENCE BY CAOOY

ACTION PLAN
for Childhood Behavioral Conditions
INFORMATIONAL GUIDE FOR PARENTS

Bio-Assessment Recommendations
Follow these steps to assist in
discovering the causation of a
Childhood Behavioral Condition.

CAOOY: Coalition Against
Overmedicating Our Youth
2012

Nutritional Intervention
- Meet with a nutritionist for a nutrient deficiency assessment
- Learn about the benefits of whole food nutrition for children

Considerations:
- Limit/ eliminate processed foods and drinks
- Limit sugar intake/ sodas / diet sodas and juices
- Eliminate gluten
- Include healthy fats, such as purified Omega- 3 fish oil supplement
- Include quality proteins
- Include naturally colored vegetables containing powerful phyto-antioxidants
- Include some fruits
- Buy organic fruits and vegetables if possible
- Increase purified water to 1 liter a day
- Increase pure psyllium fiber to 12 grams a day

Chiropractic Assessment
- Rule out cervical subluxation
- Remove spinal nerve stress and nerve interference

Digestion/Absorption/Elimination Assessment
- Obtain a nutrient deficiency assessment and GI health assessment (lab work)
- Obtain a GI health and nutritional status bio-assessment and correct as needed prior to removing toxins from the body
- Obtain a Bio-energy feedback scan

Cognitive Behavior Therapy (C.B.T.) Intervention
- Focused Guided Imagery or Visualization techniques to help train the child's mind, increasing a positive thought process
- Obtain therapy from a therapist that is specialized in Rational Emotive Behavior Therapy

Tutoring
- Meet with teacher and/or reading specialist to assess if tutoring is necessary or helpful
- Decide which type of tutoring would be best including: school-provided tutoring, peer tutoring, parental tutoring, and/or private tutoring

Ophthalmic Assessment/ Auditory Assessment
- Obtain a complete evaluation by a developmental optometrist, also known as a behavioral optometrist or pediatric ophthalmologist, regarding eyesight and vision to detect any deficient visual skills
- Meet with a speech-language pathologist who can evaluate how well a child understands and uses language, ask if further assessments are warranted
- If needed, obtain a complete evaluation by an audiologist who can assess audio processing difficulties. The actual diagnosis of an auditory processing disorder (APD), also known as central auditory processing disorder (CAPD), is made by an audiologist.
- The audiologist and speech-language pathologist may work as a team. The audiologist can help with the functional problems of hearing and processing, while the speech-language pathologist focuses on language issues.
- A child must be at least 7 or 8 years old for the APD assessment

**Review Drug Therapy Monitoring Protocols/
Differential Diagnosing for Children Currently
on Medication:**
- Review drug regimen by an experienced pharmacist specializing in ADD stimulant and psychiatric medications
- Parent and child should understand complete side effect profile of drug therapy as well as drug monitoring protocols
- Discuss drug regimen with a physician specializing in differential diagnosing to rule out underlying causation of behavioral symptoms due to nutritional, physiological and environmental risk factors
- Recommended reading reference: *Over Medicating Our Youth: The Public Awareness Guide for ADD and Psychiatric Medications*

*Provided by the CAOOY:
Coalition Against Overmedicating Our Youth*

Steps to Follow for Childhood ADD and Mental Illness Symptoms

Contact a Physician

1. Contact a physician specializing in differential diagnosis to rule out causation of the behavioral condition.
2. The physician should be responsible to evaluate all results from the bio-assessment recommendations in this Action Plan.
3. The child's parent or guardian should obtain C.B.T., nutritional, chiropractic, bio-energy feedback and learning assessments.

Treatment Plan

1. The physician should outline a treatment plan that allows a time frame for bio-assessment interventions to help reverse behavioral symptoms.
2. The physician should determine a time frame for implementing drug therapy if bio-assessment interventions are not achieving therapeutic results.
3. Drug therapy in children should be closely monitored by a pharmacist specializing in ADD stimulant and psychiatric medication therapy to prevent long term side effects.
4. The Coalition Against Overmedicating Our Youth(CAOOY) offers free medication consultations to ensure safe and effective drug therapy in children.

What else can be done?
Ask questions
Contact CAOOY
for free recommendations
and consultations at
www.CAOOY.org

The mission of the Coalition Against Overmedicating Our Youth is to provide free medication consultations as well as bio-assessment recommendations for children with behavioral symptoms prior to drug therapy. Additionally, the Coalition provides safe and effective medication monitoring protocols for children requiring drug therapy.

Connect with the Coalition Against Overmedicating Our Youth:

/CAOOYorg

/CAOOYorg

in/FrankGranett

C.A.O.O.Y.
Coalition Against Overmedicating Our Youth
World Advocate for Children ©

DIFFERENTIAL DIAGNOSIS PROTOCOL
FOR CHILDREN AGES 4–18

- Recommend history and physical evaluation conducted by an independent Medical Doctor. Include extensive assessment of the patient's nutritional, physiological, and environmental status relevant to the presentation of the ADHD or psychiatric condition while considering a differential diagnosis. The psychiatrist shall receive all records and results of the Medical Doctor's assessment.

- Recommend Medical Doctor inform child's parent of Cognitive Behavioral Therapy intervention programs during the first six months of medical assessment. For example, Rational Emotive Behavioral Therapy (R.E.B.T.) which helps a child stop and think about feelings and consequences of a response. This therapy is effective in a child as he or she learns to examine positive and negative outcomes associated with a particular solution.

- Recommend Medical Doctor inform parent or guardian to implement a nutritional program void of chemicals, allergens, food flavorings, colorings as well as processed foods during the course of evaluation. Drug therapy intervention should not be initiated unless patient is non-responsive to alternative treatment plans for a minimum of six months.

If patient history and physical involves head trauma, recommend an updated S.P.E.C.T. or D.T.I. scan to rule out physiological etiology for the behavioral condition.

- Recommend physician inform parent or guardian to have child tested for toxicology assessment via Spectravision Bio-energy feedback scanning to rule out excessive toxins, including pesticides from food sources and phthalates from plastic water bottles which may contribute to the behavioral condition.

- Recommend heavy metal toxicity assessment via urine porphyrin test only if Spectravision scan is negative.

- Recommend parasite assessment via stool sample, immunoassay and parasitic blood testing to rule out False/Negative parasite results. This testing is critical as over 85 percent of children harbor some form of undiagnosed parasitic infection. Recommend testing by a qualified parasitologist for accurate diagnosis.
- Recommend Omega-3 index blood test to rule out EPA and DHA essential fatty acid deficiency.
- Recommend Chiropractic care assessment by a highly qualified chiropractic or osteopathic physician. Rule out impinged or blocked nervous system energy flow from the spine to stomach and intestines. Since the stomach and small intestine produce neurotransmitter precursors for cognitive and executive function, this assessment should be conducted immediately. The Brain-gut Connection involves the importance of optimum nervous system energy flow to the stomach and intestines, ensuring the production of critical neurotransmitters for positive childhood behavioral development. (Reference Brain-gut Connection diagram, Chapter 8.
- Recommend physician inform parent or guardian progress of the aforementioned assessments. If these interventions do not significantly improve the behavioral condition, then medication therapy may be suggested only upon consent of the parent or guardian.
- Recommend medication therapy at low starting doses to be gradually titrated if positive response is not achieved. More than two psychoactive medications are not recommended in children during the course of a drug therapy treatment plan.

The Informed Consent Document for ADHD and Psychiatric Medications shall be signed by the physician and parent or guardian prior to issuance of new prescription of ADHD stimulant or psychiatric drug therapy.

STIMULANT MEDICATION THERAPY

- Recommend the Differential Diagnosis Protocol for children 4–18 years of age.
- Recommend a comprehensive differential diagnosis by a Medical Doctor prior to initiating stimulant drug therapy.
- Recommend physician complete a baseline E.K.G. and cardiac enzyme blood test for the child prior to stimulant drug therapy. Cardiac function tests shall be repeated in three month and six month intervals, then once a year thereafter.
- Recommend height and weight monitoring every three months.
- Recommend office visit once monthly to monitor patient's cardiac function prior to issuance of new prescription. Post -dating prescriptions for convenience to eliminate office visit is not recommended.
- Recommend child's vital signs including blood pressure, pulse and heart rate checked once a month prior to issuance of new stimulant prescription.

Stimulant drug therapy should not be recommended in children less than seven years old. These drugs include, and not limited to, Adderall, Ritalin, Focalin, Concerta, Metadate, and Vyvanse as well as their generic alternatives.

- Recommend immediate discontinuance of a drug, if cardiac function is compromised during course of therapy.
- Recommend ADHD stimulant therapy not be immediately discontinued in a non-emergency, during course of therapy.
- Recommend taper down drug over a period of four months for drug therapy longer than one year duration. Recommend taper down drug over a period of two months for drug therapy shorter than one year duration.
- Recommend short acting stimulant therapy doses administered at least six hours apart and not more than two doses per 24 hour period.

- Recommend immediate re-evaluation of stimulant drug therapy and contact physician if the following symptoms occur:
  1. Pronounced aggressive behavior or hostility
  2. Pronounced bipolar depression
  3. Pronounced thought problems
  4. Development of new psychotic symptoms i.e. hearing voices, manic episodes, and believing things that are not true.
  5. Indications of cardiac abnormalities i.e. chest pain, shortness of breath, chronic headaches and fainting.
- Recommend no Over-the-counter (OTC) and prescription decongestants while on ADHD stimulant therapy.
- Recommend a consultation with your physician and pharmacist regarding all prior to starting ADHD stimulant drug therapy as some medications may interact with stimulant drug therapy.
- Recommend a comprehensive discussion with your child's doctor involving a complete medical history including thyroid disease, visual/auditory perception conditions, seizures, liver and kidney disease, cardiac disease, and mental illness involving depression, psychosis, and mania.
- Recommend no stimulant drug therapy while pregnant
- Recommend continuance of alternative treatment plans including Cognitive Behavioral Therapy while child is taking stimulant drug therapy.

Side effects of ADHD stimulant drug therapy include, not limited to:

1. Reduced growth involving height and weight
2. Blurred vision
3. Dizziness
4. Decreased appetite
5. Seizures, primarily in patients with seizure history
6. Sleep disorders
7. Nervousness and stomach ache

Stimulant drug therapy may affect driving ability. Contact your doctor if side effects are chronic and do not subside.

Possible cardiac related dysfunction with stimulant drug therapy

- Sudden cardiac death
- Increased blood pressure and heart rate

PSYCHIATRIC MEDICATION THERAPY

Recommend a comprehensive differential diagnosis by an independent medical doctor prior to initiating psychiatric drug therapy in children.

- Psychiatric medications should not be prescribed in children younger than fourteen years old without clinical rationale eliminating nutritional, physiological or environmental etiology of the behavioral condition.
- Recommend and monitor complete enzyme blood panel including liver and cardiac enzymes prior to implementing a psychiatric medication treatment plan in children.
- Recommend and monitor Complete Blood Count (CBC) including White Blood Count during the first month of drug treatment and every three month thereafter for assessment of Leukopenia, Neutropenia, and Agranulocytosis.
- Recommend not to prescribe atypical anti-psychotic medications under the age of sixteen.

History and physical exam should assess the following prior to prescribing psychiatric medications:

1. Seizures
2. Cardiac disease
3. Liver disease
4. Thyroid disease
5. Diabetes

6. Blood disorders
7. Elevated prolactin levels

- Recommend no psychiatric drug therapy while pregnant.
- Recommend no alcohol while taking psychiatric drugs.
- Recommend no O.T.C. decongestants, cough suppressants and antihistamines while taking psychiatric drugs
- Recommend immediate re-evaluation of psychiatric therapy and contact physician if the following occurs:
  1. Panic attacks
  2. Severe agitation
  3. Muscular rigidity
  4. High fever
  5. Suicide thoughts
  6. Attempting suicide
  7. Insomnia
  8. Severe depression
  9. Low White Blood Cell count

Psychiatric medications may cause the following diseases:

- Diabetes—Monitor excessive thirst, hunger, urination, fatigue, confusion, or fruity breath smell.
- Hyperlipidemia—Monitor complete cholesterol panel including Low Density Lipoprotein (LDL), High Density Lipoprotein (HDL), and triglycerides. Obtain blood baseline level prior to psychiatric therapy and monitor every three months thereafter.
- Neuroleptic Malignant Syndrome (NMS)—Monitor the following symptom and contact doctor as this syndrome may lead to sudden death. a) High fever b) Stiff or rigid muscles c) Profuse sweating d) Changes in heart rate, pulse, and blood pressure
- Tardive dyskinesia—Contact physician immediately if uncontrolled movements occur in the face, or other body parts.

- Orthostatic hypotension—Contact physician if fainting occurs from rising from a resting position due to a sudden decrease in blood pressure.
- Seizures—Contact physician immediately if seizures develop during course of therapy.

Side Effects of psychiatric drug therapies include but not limited to:

-

- Nausea
- Fatigue
- Weight gain
- Tachycardia
- Increased appetite
- Dizziness
- Dry mouth
- Sore throat
- Vomiting
- Constipation

SUICIDE PREVENTION

Upon initiation of ADHD stimulant or psychiatric drug therapy, family members and patients should closely monitor changes in behavior, mood, as well as suicidal thoughts. Any sudden change in the aforementioned must be immediately communicated to the physician.

All future doctor appointments should be scheduled every thirty five days for the most prudent monitoring practices in children.

Atypical anti-psychotic medications include the following as well as their generic alternatives:

– Zyprexa – Geodon – Seroquel – Latuda – Clozaril – Saphris – Abilify – Invega – Risperdal

Haldol and Fanapt

Typical anti-psychotic medications include the following as well as their generic alternatives:

– Mellaril – Thorazine – Navane – Stelazine – Trilafon

Voluntary Side Effect or Adverse Drug Reaction Reporting to the FDA:
1-800-FDA-0178 to fax a report
1-800-FDA-1088 to report by phone
www.FDA.gov/medwatch/report.htm to report online

The Action Plan for Childhood Behavioral Conditions
Website: www.CAOOY.org "Ask the Pharmacist" for free consultations
Email: FrankGranett@CAOOY.org

Notes

_____
_____
_____
_____
_____
_____
_____
_____
_____
_____
_____
_____
_____
_____
_____
_____
_____
_____
_____
_____
_____

Ask the Pharmacist • www.CAOOY.org

Helping Determine Causation
of Behavioral Conditions

Donations Provide
Free Clinical Bio-Assesment
and Medication Consultations

CAOOY
Coalition Against Overmedicating Our Youth
WORLD   ADVOCATE   FOR   CHILDREN©

CHAPTER 7

Suicide Prevention

"Don't grieve for me, for now I'm free, I'm following the path God laid
    for me.

I took His hand when I heard his call, I turned by back and left it all.

I could not stay another day, To laugh, to love, to work, or to play.

Tasks left undone must stay that way, I've found that peace at the end of
    the day.

If my parting has left a void, then fill it with remembered joy.

A friendship shared, a laugh, a kiss, Ah yes, these things too I will miss.

Be not burdened with times of sorrow, I wish you the sunshine of tomorrow.

My life's been full, I savored much, Good friends, good times, a loved
    one's touch.

Perhaps my time seemed all too brief, Don't lengthen it now with
    undue grief.

Lift up your heart and share with me, God wanted me now. He set me free."

In Loving Memory of Jeremiah

Entered Life 9/10/1991

Entered eternal life 11/12/2011

Jeremiah was an unmistakable positive free spirit brought into this world, and prematurely taken away from all who knew him. His love of life was vibrant and intense. With dance moves like Michael Jackson, Jeremiah was the life of the party. He was in constant motion. Happy times were always guaranteed when Jeremiah came to our doorstep. Academically and in sports, he focused on achieving a place in college athletics. Jeremiah was a fierce competitor. With so many positives going for him, why did he have inner mental pain and despair? ....despair and helplessness to the point of taking his presence away from earth.

Jeremiah's story, in many respects, is similar to thousands of teenagers and young adults in the United States, as well as beyond its borders. During the last year of his life, Jeremiah battled bipolar depression after taking anti-seizure medications for the majority of his youth. He developed seizures at age twelve after a traumatic head-to-head collision during a very competitive travel league soccer game. The collision was so forceful that a loud crack-like sound was heard, clear across other soccer field. Jeremiah, being the fierce competitor, kept playing while the other player fell crashing to the ground and was rushed to a nearby hospital for emergency treatment.

Approximately three months later, Jeremiah developed a seizure condition. During his high school years, he experienced multiple concussive sport injuries, further magnifying his original traumatic brain injury at age twelve. His primary seizure treatment included the anticonvulsant drug, Keppra, which kept him stable until age nineteen...a time in his life when his eternal life path began.

The question is...why was Jeremiah taken at the hands of suicide after multiple concussive injuries due to a significant brain injury at age twelve. The facts are more conclusive today regarding a greater percentage of traumatic brain injury patients will die from suicide than the regular population. Especially in the child population, significant brain injury should be aggressively monitored for the first ten years following the injury. This information is now beginning to be released to the general population as well as all healthcare professionals caring for children with behavioral challenges.

At age nineteen, his bipolar diagnosis surfaced. His mental illness condition was treated primarily with drug intervention, void of a differential diagnosis, physiological assessment and alternative treatment plans. His physiological status for past closed head injury was not fully assessed according to his treatment plan. Response to various antidepressant medications, including Lexapro, would exacerbate Jeremiah's condition. Manufacturer guidelines recommend extreme caution using Lexapro in patients with a history of seizure disorder. Furthermore, Lexapro is a very potent selective serotonin reuptake inhibitor with hundred times the potency of the R-enantiomer drug Celexa, with inhibition of 5-HT reuptake into neuronal cells. Toxic side effects, including serotonin syndrome or neuroleptic malignant syndrome in seizure patients are possible with Lexapro and other antidepressants within the same pharmacological class.

In desperation, psychiatrists began prescribing the powerful atypical antipsychotic medications, which further created a downward spiral. These medications help many patients with debilitating psychiatric disorders. However, a complete history and physiological assessment by an independent medical doctor should be mandated prior to atypical psychotropic drug treatment in children and young adults with past closed head injuries.

As discussed in chapter 3, regarding the assessment of physiological factors contributing to behavioral symptoms, children should receive a comprehensive physiological assessment to determine cause of the condition. This process should be completed by a highly qualified physician specializing in childhood behavior conditions. A physical assessment of the entire spinal column should be initiated to rule out subluxation or dislocation of the vertebrae. Furthermore, research confirms that closed head injuries if not appropriately assessed and treated can lead to minor depression as well as bipolar depression.

Reforms in the physiological assessment of children as recommended in the Action Plan for Childhood Behavioral Conditions would have offered insight to possible cause of his bipolar condition. The physiological, nutritional, and environmental factors would have provided a more focused direction in his treatment plan.

Jeremiah would have good days, and bad days, never letting his peers realize the bad. Nondrug therapy interventions and a differential diagnosis protocol as set forth in the Action Plan for Childhood Behavioral Conditions were to begin prior to the holiday season of 2011. Additionally, a toxicology analysis via Spectravision Bio-energy feedback scanning would determine whether Jeremiah retained excessive toxins within the body contributing to his state of mind. Toxins could have accumulated over the years since his blunt head injury may have damaged his blood–brain barrier system, which provides the transport system for nourishment and protects the brain internally from toxins, as the skull protects the brain externally.

Diffusion Tensor Imaging, a specialized form of MRI, was scheduled to rule out a physiological condition due to his past head trauma at age twelve…. It was too late. Jeremiah was taken from this earth for a cause:

- A cause to make people around the world take notice of children in pain, mental anguish, mental turmoil and inner restlessness so devastating, wanting to end their suffering without notice
- A cause to mandate a differential diagnosis prior to prescribing ADHD and psychiatric medications
- A cause to reform excessive psychiatric drug prescribing in children and young adults
- A cause to implement comprehensive physiological assessments to rule out underlying causation of behavioral conditions
- A cause to mandate psychological counseling prior to medicating young children
- A cause for the Department of Health and Human Services in Washington DC to mandate the Informed Consent Document for ADHD and Psychiatric Medications by all physicians treating children and young adults with stimulant and psychiatric medications

Young adults age eighteen and older must be allowed to obtain legal representation by their parents if behavioral crisis symptoms incapacitate the child. The current informed consent law regarding the administration of psychotropic drug therapy for patients aged eighteen and older protects institutions, drug manufacturers, as well as physicians. The patient at this age should be allowed parental representation for treatment plan decisions.

Jeremiah's purpose on this earth was to make people laugh and feel good about one another. He was a great lifelong friend, like a brother to my son. Two hours before Jeremiah was taken from this earth, he messaged my son on his Facebook wall "Happy twenty-first birthday... to my brother, see you soon!"

On November 12, 2011, Jeremiah's spirit touched those he knew without his presence of body. His vibrant spirit is more evident today than ever before.

Although suicide awareness is now a heightened priority in many high schools across America, an action plan with specified objectives for parents and children with behavioral conditions requires implementation to eliminate teenage suicide. Teenagers and young adults do not choose suicide.....suicide is the end result of a dysfunctional mental health system lacking the appropriate clinical assessment options to find cause of major depression prior to premature drug therapy.

Since his tragic death in November 2011, hundreds of people gather once a year and run the "Jeremiah mile" on a track where he escaped his inner pain of severe depression and harmful thoughts.....a track where he would finish a race in victory and smile at his fans in the stands.....a track which would lead him to a college scholarship. Jeremiah was a special human motivator. Jeremiah's creator took him from this earth to motivate others battling severe behavioral challenges. Jeremiah is asking each one of us to become motivated and demand reform.....giving children and young adults a voice to have this reform implemented.

My 17 year old daughter, Brooke, explains how she felt about the presence and loss of Jeremiah, through her high school English paper.

When your tank is empty

Losing a loved one to suicide is a very traumatic experience. The feeling of loss creates emptiness, sometimes so difficult to overcome. I try to understand the suicide tragedy of my brother's best friend, Jeremiah. As a second big brother, he taught me how to focus and achieve my goals in life. Jeremiah was a great person. He united all kids in our high school. He always had a smile. His dedication and focus to his favorite sport of running track earned him a college scholarship. I was so proud of him for achieving one of his goals in life. Although Jeremiah lost his battle, to bipolar depression, his life lessons that he taught will stay with me forever. The summer before he passed, Jeremiah made a profound statement... "When your tank is empty just keep going...it's all in your mind."

My four sisters and I always looked forward to the summer with Jeremiah. My brother Robert returned home from Ferris State University. Now we had two big brothers to look up to and had fun all summer long. Robert and Jeremiah would train for their upcoming fall sport season...Jeremiah in track, and my brother Robert goaltending for Ferris State. Their training sessions were always intense. My sisters and I would always go on morning runs with Jeremiah. One morning, in particular, I will never forget.

We were half way through a long run. The sun's rays beaming down on our faces creating drops of sweat rolling down our faces like a waterfall. I was exhausted, my legs felt like jello. Each step felt like I was lifting a huge amount of weight. I felt like my body was over heating. As I continued to run, each step I was slowing down. My legs gave out and dropped to the hard cement. I lied down on the hot cement, realizing I could not get up to finish the last stretch back to my house. Jeremiah ran over to me.

"Brooke get up, you can do it! Believe in yourself." He exclaimed.

"I can't Jeremiah. I am tired." I said.

At that moment he said a profound statement that will stick with me forever. "When your tank is empty just keep going it's all in your mind." Jeremiah said. He picked me up; we slowly started to run back to my house to finish that long stretch. He took his hands and pushed my back behind me to keep me going. At that moment, through his inspiration, I kept going until we made it back to my house, and almost beat him! During the past two summers, I miss Jeremiah being part of our extended family. I will always remember that day running in my subdivision, when I could run no further. That moment of continuing on, even though it hurt, helps me endure my day to day challenges. Jeremiah picked me up saying those powerful words.

Every day that I think of Jeremiah, there are no tears anymore. There is always a smile on my face. There is no time to grieve anymore, it is time to celebrate his life and "live life to the fullest" as he would say. The impact that he has made on my life is extraordinary. The experiences he shared with my family are memories that will be in our hearts forever. To this day, I always put my best effort into everything I do. Yes, there will be days where I want to give up.....but my tank is never empty, it is all in my mind.

Policymakers in Washington, DC, including Senator Carper from Delaware, recognize the immediate need for reform. Psychiatrists across America are now speaking out, demanding reform within their own governing body of the American Psychiatric Association. The Director of National Institute of Mental Health in Washington DC states the current assessment process for mental disorders "lacks validity". Specifically, a reformation of the Diagnostic and Statistical Manual of Mental Disorders requires a more comprehensive assessment approach in the treatment of children with behavioral conditions.

Educators, parents, and healthcare professionals should recognize the need for mandated Cognitive Behavioral Therapy (CBT) programs as well as focused guided visualization programs for children prior to prematurely medicating our youth. CBT defines specific objectives for a child's behavioral condition and uses individualized psychotherapy interventions to achieve positive behavioral outcomes.

Mental health education should be implemented in Public and private schools. For decades, physical strength training has been taught in schools. Why are school districts waiting for the next school shootings to implement mental health strength training programs? Teenagers should understand how to develop a positive emotion thought process. CBT programs with highly qualified psychotherapists should be offered in high schools across America.

School districts should require CBT programs as a mandate even if stimulant or psychiatric drug therapy has been chosen as the treatment plan for children with behavioral symptoms. Additionally, a strict whole-foods nutritional program should be required while a child completes a differential diagnosis for ADHD and psychiatric conditions to determine cause of the behavior.

Suicide prevention initiatives are becoming stronger day by day, giving parents and educators the tools they need to help children and young adults win the battle against suicide. Teenagers and young adults do not choose to commit suicide....suicide is the end result involving undiagnosed or misdiagnosed causation of emotional pain...emotional pain that envelopes and controls thought processes...emotional pain that drug therapy alone cannot regulate.

Stimulant and psychiatric drug therapy intervention should not be implemented until the cause of emotional pain has been assessed. Children with inner emotional pain, so devastating as to sacrifice their life, should have the right to receive a comprehensive nutritional, physiological, and environmental assessment while completing a differential diagnosis by their physician.

School administrators should encourage students to post suicide awareness meetings within their schools. The American Foundation for Suicide Prevention (AFSP) is a nonprofit foundation, which provides a wealth of information and workshops for the prevention of suicide. AFSP supports research to improve the public's understanding of suicide and its prevention. The organization also provides education and information about depression and suicide to professionals, the media, and the public through workshops and training.

Additionally, AFSP provides programs to survivors of suicide loss that can be of assistance and involves survivors in suicide prevention. The primary AFSP survivor initiatives include the National Survivors of Suicide Day program, which is broadcast to over 175 communities and simulcast on its Web site as well as the Survivor e-Network. Their stated purpose is "to understand and prevent suicide through research, education and advocacy, and to reach out to people with mental disorders and those impacted by suicide".[30]

Another effective organization to help prevent suicide in teens is called the Yellow Ribbon organization. The Yellow Ribbon Suicide Prevention Program is a very effective community based program developed to combat teenage suicide through public awareness involving education and training. Yellow Ribbon helps communities as well as schools identify resources for specific plans of action. The BE-A-Link suicide prevention gatekeeper training and ASK 4 Help suicide prevention training teach the critical warning signs for suicide. Knowing these factors can help lead to early intervention and help save lives.

The Yellow Ribbon organization began in response to the death of Mike Emme, founders Dar and Dale Emme's son, in 1994. Words of inspiration and help were placed on a bright yellow paper and shared with teenagers at his funeral service. Teenagers shared the messages locally and began to mail them to friends and family. Within three weeks, word came of a girl saved after she asked for help using this bright yellow message, the hallmark of the program - the Ask 4 Help Card. Yellow Ribbon is now an internationally recognized influence to help teens prevent suicide.

SUICIDE RISKS

Psychiatric Disorders:
- At least 90 percent of people who die from suicide have a diagnosable and treatable psychiatric illness, including major depression, bipolar depression or other depressive illnesses including Schizophrenia, alcohol or drug abuse in combination with depression.
- Posttraumatic Stress Disorder, or some other anxiety disorder, Bulimia or anorexia nervosa
- Personality disorders, especially borderline or antisocial.

Past History of Attempted Suicide:
- Between 20 and 50 percent of people who die from suicide had previously attempted suicide. Those who have made serious

suicide attempts are at a much higher risk for actually taking their lives.

Genetic Predisposition:
- Family history of suicide, suicide attempts, depression or other psychiatric illness

Neurotransmitters:
- A clear relationship has been demonstrated between low concentrations of the serotonin metabolite 5-hydroxyindoleacetic acid (5-HIAA) in cerebrospinal fluid and an increased incidence of attempted and completed suicide in psychiatric patients.

Impulsivity:
- Impulsive individuals are more apt to act on suicidal impulses.

Demographics:
- Sex: Males are three to five times more likely to die by suicide than females.
- Age: Elderly Caucasian males have the highest suicide rates.

Traumatic Brain Injury (TBI):
- Patients with TBI should be monitored at least ten years after the original brain injury for suicidal risk
- TBI patients have a greater risk of suicide death than the regular population
- CAOOY recommends a yearly SPECT or Diffusion Tensor Imaging brain scan to monitor changes in baseline neuro-cellular function due to brain trauma.

Suicide is the second leading cause of death among college students in the United States. A person dies from suicide every sixteen minutes and attempts suicide every one minute. How do we as a society help a person who expresses thoughts of suicide? Training workshops provide people with resources to help prevent suicide. However, it becomes critical for many people surrounding a loved one to communicate the immediate need for intervention and appropriate treatment to help effectively restore a person's emotional state of mind.

Local crisis centers provide immediate assistance for suicide; however, the National Suicide Prevention Hotline (800 273-TALK) has experienced crisis professionals to answer calls and effectively direct your loved one to immediate care. Mental illness in children should require the utilization of infinite resources to help determine underlying causation of behavioral symptoms. Physicians, therapists, educators, and parents should work together as one body of diverse knowledge, specified in the Action Plan for Childhood Behavioral Conditions. This action plan represents the steps needed to help parents determine the cause of harmful thought processes. The Coalition Against Overmedicating Our Youth is a non-profit organization that assists parents, educators, and physicians by counseling children's medication profiles for prudent use, while offering alternative assessments as stated in the Action Plan for Childhood Behavioral Conditions.

The education system in America is currently biased toward stimulant drug therapy, as the primary intervention in children to control behavioral symptoms. Stimulant drug therapy, in many cases, controls behavioral symptoms in a relatively short period of time. However, the long-term harmful side effects including anxiety, minor depression and bipolar depression as stated in the FDA Med Guide alert warrants an immediate change of action. Educators, parents and healthcare professionals should realize that ADHD stimulant drug therapy over a period of time may cause a child to develop minor depression, bipolar depression, as well as anxiety.

This cycle of drug therapy is a contributing factor in the behavioral health crisis in America involving our youth. The rapid escalation of teenage and young adult suicide in the United States may be directly linked to this socially accepted drug cycle. Parents, educators, and physicians should consider the implementation of the Action Plan for Childhood Behavioral Conditions as well as an established alliance with the Coalition Against Overmedicating Our Youth to prevent teen suicide.

The first step in suicide prevention is to effectively reform the assessment and treatment plan in children with behavioral conditions. Psychotherapy and the bio-assessments recommended in the Action Plan for Childhood Behavioral Conditions should be referred to parents by the education system. Furthermore, a team approach to therapy should be implemented, wherein all treatment disciplines communicate on the appropriateness of the assessment and primary treatment plan.

Teachers are employed by the education system for the purpose of educating our children. They have one of the most important occupations that guide our youth. Unfortunately, they are constrained in their teaching efforts due to childhood behavioral conditions. In the short term, teachers can offer observational guidance regarding a child's behavioral treatment plan. In doing so, less drug intervention and more therapy as well as differential diagnosing will revert the child to normal behavioral without long-term side effects of drug therapy.

I receive many questions from parents on the issue for or against medicating their children exhibiting behavioral conditions. This decision can be made only by parents. The stress in making this decision may be mitigated by knowing the facts. Parents need to become more informed regarding the advances in alternative treatment plans and bio-assessments prior to making this important decision.

With the assistance of educators and the Coalition Against Overmedicating Our Youth, parents will be in a much better position to help their child revert to normal behavior. This process requires patience and time. I have consulted with many parents prior to them medicating their child. As long as parents have perseverance and the long-term behavioral health goals for their children in sight, successful treatment is possible.

Psychotherapy conducted by highly qualified professionals with a positive track record should be the first line of intervention. Nutritional, physiological, and environmental factors can be immediately assessed by a qualified physician during the initial differential diagnosis period. Parents should take ownership of this process for the long-term health of their child. Effective guidance from educators and Coalition Against Overmedicating Our Youth will allow this process to slow the drug cycle and help parents determine cause of their child's behavioral condition.

Education curriculum changes for students could be implemented to understand the long-term consequences of ignoring the causation of behavioral symptoms in children. Health classes at the freshman high school level could include a semester involving mental health strengthening classes for behavioral conditions. The more children understand their mind and body, the more they can help themselves heal during a behavioral health crisis. Two courses I highly recommend for the freshman high school curriculum would include focus-guided visualization and rational emotive behavior therapy (REBT).

As I discuss in chapter 9, focus-guided visualization is practiced by elite athletes around the world to strengthen the mind, thought processes, as well as self-confidence. REBT, a form of cognitive behavioral therapy, teaches children how to be accountable for behavioral actions. Techniques are utilized in teaching these therapies.

Ultimately, the objective of the Coalition Against Overmedicating Our Youth is to assist parents, educators as well as healthcare professionals to help children regain normal behavioral development without long term side effects of drug therapy. Teachers will once again be able to instruct without the constraints of childhood behavioral conditions and suicide awareness will no longer be an issue in high schools across America.

Notes

_____

_____

_____

_____

_____

_____

_____

_____

_____

_____

_____

_____

_____

_____

_____

_____

_____

_____

_____

Ask the Pharmacist • www.CAOOY.org

Helping Determine Causation of Behavioral Conditions

Donations Provide Free Clinical Bio-Assesment and Medication Consultations

CAOOY

Coalition Against Overmedicating Our Youth

WORLD ADVOCATE FOR CHILDREN®

CHAPTER 8

How to Develop a Healthy Mind

The brain is the most complex organ system of the human body. With an intricate communication system involving neuronal cells, and multiple forms of chemical neurotransmitters, the brain efficiently transmits impulses involved in cognitive function relative to the presentation of child behavior. These impulses generated to effectively transmit cognitive function in childhood behavioral development are essential to the advancement of the healthy mind.

Many critical factors are necessary for the advancement of a healthy mind as a child proceeds in their developmental stages of life. A child must develop efficient digestive and toxin elimination organ systems including the liver, gallbladder, kidney, small intestine, and large intestine. Elimination of toxic nutrition and toxic environmental exposure is essential. Good nutrition is critical. In the words of Hippocrates, "Let food be thy medicine and let thy medicine be thy food."

According to the American Journal of Clinical Nutrition, there is an increased recognition and need of polyunsaturated fatty acids in health promotion, especially in defense of ADHD and psychiatric disorders. Studies of the postmortem brain in psychiatric patients show significant depletion of polyunsaturated fatty acids within the red blood cell membranes of the prefrontal cortex.[31]

The prefrontal cortex of the brain is the primary center for cognitive function. This polyunsaturated fatty acid depletion in the cortex of psychiatric patients provides rationale for the supplementation of omega-3 fatty acids, or fish oil, in patients assessed with behavioral disorders. The normal brain tissue is composed of sixty-five percent lipids and approximately eight percent comprises omega fatty acids including eicosapentaenoic acid (EPA). Dr. Ralph Holman, researcher in fatty acids, from the University of Minnesota who gave omega-3 its name, states that EPA is the primary essential fatty acid responsible for neurological function.[32]

EPA possesses membrane-enhancing properties within neuronal cells of the brain by increasing dopaminergic neurotransmission, which is essential to the development of childhood cognitive behavioral function. Most importantly, EPA helps repair oxidative damage of brain cells due to psychiatric disease or toxic exposure, and promotes neuronal cell growth.

In a six-month study involving patients with schizophrenia and Huntington's disease who were treated with the essential fatty acid EPA or a placebo, the placebo group had clearly lost cerebral tissue growth while the patients receiving the EPA supplementation had a significant increase in gray and white brain matter.[33]

Further support of EPA nutrient supplementation involves recent research in mice. This research provides conclusive insight into these essential fatty acids positively altering the brain's functionality. Nature Neuroscience of Scientific American published significant studies regarding the importance of essential fatty acids in the brain.

The research group led by Dr. Mathieu Lafourcade of the French National Institute for Health and Medical Research Neurocenter in France found that mice reared on an omega-3-deficient diet exhibited a wide range of depressive symptoms in behavioral testing. The deficient mice, for example, gave up more easily in a forced swimming test, were less inclined to explore, and were more inclined to stay near the wall of the cage, which is a widely accepted index of anxiety or mood disorder. Dr. Lafourcade stated, "Our results can now corroborate clinical and epidemiological studies which have revealed associations between omega-3 imbalance and mood disorders".[34]

Depletion of essential fatty acid composition of the brain may compromise effective psychoneuroendocrine function. Psychoneuroendocrine function involves fluctuations of bio-chemicals including dopamine, norepinephrine and adrenalin, and how these fluctuations affect human behavior as well as cognitive thought processes. Over the counter fish oil supplementation and food sources rich in omega-3 fatty acids including fish, egg products, avocados and walnuts are important dietary considerations in children that exhibit ADHD or psychiatric behavioral conditions. However, the heavy metal, mercury, is a toxin with large concentrations in fish. Limit your child's intake of fish and obtain dietary EPA from mercury-free omega-3 as well as walnuts, avocados and eggs. Purchase walnuts encased in their shell to avoid toxic chemical sprays used in the packaging of unshelled walnuts.

The aforementioned studies show that the EPA in fish oil can provide mood-stabilizing properties in psychiatric conditions and is a safe supplement used as directed in children and young adults. Additionally, the differential diagnosis assessment of children who exhibit ADHD or psychiatric behavior should be tested for EPA deficiency.

The omega-3 index blood test measures the percentage of docosahexaenoic acid as well as EPA essential fatty acids in the blood. The omega-3 index blood test is a necessary diagnostic assay in the differential diagnosis protocol in the Action Plan for Childhood Behavioral Conditions.

Since EPA is not manufactured in the body, supplementation and nutritional sources are essential to the development of a child's healthy mind. When selecting an over the counter omega-3 fatty acid fish oil supplement, be sure that the manufacturer has quality standards, which remove trace heavy metal toxins including mercury, lead, nickel, cadmium, and arsenic during the extraction process. For example, Nature's Bounty odorless fish oil gel capsules are free of toxic heavy metals due to an extensive purification process. This brand is also free of artificial colorings, flavorings, yeast, and lactose. At 1,200 mg per capsule, teenagers may take one capsule with breakfast and dinner, while children may take one capsule daily at dinner.

Other nutritional considerations in children with ADHD and psychiatric conditions involve protecting the body from mal-absorption and depletion of nutrients to promote development of the healthy mind. Mal-absorption is the inability to properly digest and absorb nutrients from food or supplements into the bloodstream. Mal-absorption also is an important consideration in cellular enzyme and antioxidant deficiency. Without complete production of enzymes as well as antioxidants, neurotransmitters are not effectively produced and may lead to the presentation of behavioral conditions.

A very prominent gastrointestinal disorder due to chronic mal-absorption is called leaky gut syndrome. This condition is characterized by damage or erosion to the intestinal lining. Without a proper diagnosis, this condition in children will manifest itself as other chronic illnesses including eczema, immune dysfunction, anxiety, irritability, chronic fatigue, intestinal distress, and joint pain.

Good nutrition and absorption into the blood stream is essential for the building blocks of neurotransmitters as well as the protection of brain tissue. Dopamine is a neurotransmitter that depends on a functional gut (stomach) flora. The dopamine neurotransmitter is necessary for a healthy mind to promote positive cognitive function thereby preventing the onset of ADHD, depression and addictive behavioral symptoms.

Critical biochemical enzymes manufactured in the gut by microorganisms are essential for the body to manufacture the neurotransmitter norepinephrine as well as dopamine. Tyrosine hydroxylase is the primary enzyme, which becomes activated in the gut by the short-chain fatty acid butyrate to produce the biochemical precursors to norepinephrine and dopamine.

Another factor for healthy mind development is the child's internal antioxidant status. The most important antioxidant of the human body to prevent toxin accumulation is glutathione. Scientists denote glutathione (GSH) as the "master" of all antioxidants that are naturally produced in the body to remove harmful disease-causing toxins. This compound is extremely effective in toxin elimination due to its sulfur-based sulfhydryl (SH) chemical group. Glutathione is a chemically putrid, odorous compound, which attracts free radical compound toxins in the body including the heavy metals mercury and arsenic.

There are thousands of toxins created in many chemically diverse forms, external and internal to the body. Long-term deficiency in eliminating toxins from a child's body may lead to cellular degeneration and eventually mask itself in chronic illness, including childhood ADHD and psychiatric behavioral conditions.

Parents should be proactive and limit exposure to toxins, including sugar, aspartame, food colorings, dyes, natural flavorings, artificial flavorings, processed/junk food, radon gas, as well as the heavy metals mercury, lead, nickel, and arsenic. If your child or a loved one is suffering from a behavioral condition, make the easy choice to assess your household food sources and remove all food toxins while converting to a whole-foods yeast-free diet plan for your child. A child's healthy mind depends on your food source intervention.

Dr. Luc Montagnier, who was awarded the 2008 Nobel Prize in Medicine, has drawn significant attention to the medicinal benefits of GSH-boosting supplementation and diet. Elevating intercellular GSH is associated with treating numerous diseases caused by excessive toxins trapped within the body. The elevation of intercellular GSH is accomplished by taking foods as well as non-denatured whey protein supplementation that provide the essential precursors to GSH. Whey protein supplementation for teenagers is a consideration for children with behavioral conditions. Use as directed and only supplement with non-denatured proteins containing no hormones, antibiotics, or pesticides on the packaging. Studies to date demonstrate that increasing GSH via dietary means has a medicinal benefit for over sixty-seven diseases.[35] These primary precursors include the amino acids cysteine, glycine, and glutamine.

Children at a very early age should be encouraged to eat the following raw, not cooked, food sources rich in GSH precursors including the following:

- Onions
- Broccoli
- Cabbage
- Cauliflower
- Watercress
- Avocado
- Spinach
- Tomatoes
- Garlic
- Asparagus

As a critical antioxidant to keep the body physically and mentally healthy, glutathione may also be supplemented with Alpha lipoic acid to keep levels high within the cells for optimal energy production, detoxification, mental health and blood sugar control.

Glutathione deficiency is more prevalent now due to a toxic food chain creating genetically dysfunctional production of genes responsible for recycling glutathione in the body. Glutathione is essential for mental health and can be tested to ensure adequate cellular levels are present in the body. Ask your physician about screening GSTP1 and GSTM1 for you or your loved one if behavioral symptoms are chronic and not responding to the other assessments as described in The Action Plan for Childhood Behavioral Conditions.

Additionally, glutathione levels have been drastically reduced in the human population during the last 40 years causing other chronic illnesses to proliferate. These illnesses include but not limited to cancer, autism, arthritis, asthma, liver disease, Alzheimer's disease, cardiac disease and chronic fatigue syndrome. Ask yourself....am I slowing down as I age? If the answer is yes, then begin the following steps to maximize your glutathione function to increase physical and mental strength.

- Eat raw, whole foods high in glutathione content
- Exercise daily, 30 to 40 minute cardiovascular training

- Supplement with high potency multivitamins and minerals as well as Alpha lipoic acid sold over the counter
- Consume a bioactive form of whey protein free of aspartame, sugar and Genetically Modified Organisms (GMO) once a day. A reputable brand of whey protein will provide children and adults the essential amino acids cysteine, glycine and glutamine for the production of glutathione.

Notice the chemical structure of glutathione in the diagram below. At the mid top potion of the compound exists HS, which is the key sulfur elemental group of glutathione. This sulf-hydryl (HS) group exhibits powerful antioxidant properties which help the body naturally eliminate free radical toxins from the body. The molecule possesses a sticky sulfurous odor.

GLUTATHIONE
Chemical structure

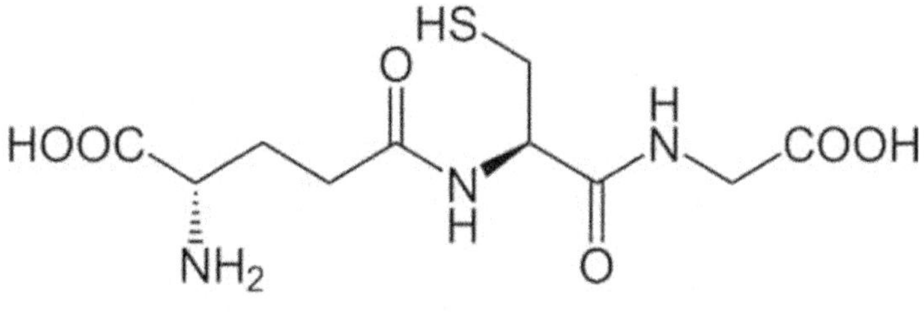

My daughters love onion wedges dipped in fresh cut avocado and diced tomatoes. Many of these combinations were tried over the years until they found what was most tasteful as well as appealing to their eyes. The key as a parent is not to fall prey to the chemical foods pandered by corporate advertisers who have no concern for your child's health.

Breakfast and after school nutritional snacks should be planned in advance while maintaining a consistent whole-foods diet plan. Snacking should involve a few of these essential raw vegetables. As you may guess, I

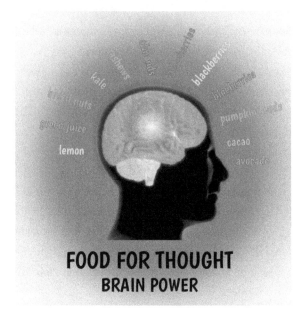

FOOD FOR THOUGHT
BRAIN POWER

am not a fan of Mac n Cheese or sugar cereals from a box with millions of dollars in corporate advertising.

A child's morning diet should consist of high protein and a small amount of complex carbohydrates. Incorporate eggs, beans, or nuts with oatmeal including fruit for breakfast. Gradually reduce a child's intake of simple carbohydrates including table sugar, white rice, and high-fructose corn syrup, while increasing complex carbohydrates such as fibrous fruits and vegetables. Over a period of time, your child will not miss the table sugar-containing food sources. Cooking more with olive and canola oil will allow children to obtain additional sources of omega-3 essential fatty acids.

Effective elimination of toxins from a child's body must occur in order for successful development of a healthy mind. A body free of toxins allows the mind to function at optimum cognitive capacity. Systems of toxin elimination involve the liver, kidney, lymphatic, blood, skin, lungs, and large intestine. Of these systems, the blood, liver, kidney, and large intestine provide the most important consideration for toxin elimination from the body.

Blood within the vascular system is the primary transporter of toxins to organ systems, which then filter the toxins for elimination from the body. The liver filters fat-soluble toxins from the blood and transports to the gallbladder for filtration and ultimately to the large intestine. Water-soluble toxins delivered to the liver, on the other hand, are primarily transported from the liver to the kidney for final elimination.

An effective home remedy for cleansing the liver involves an equal part solution of lemon juice and hot water to equal a total volume of six ounces. This solution can be consumed once a month to keep your liver filtering at optimum capacity. The gallbladder is a small pear-shaped organ located just below the liver. Its primary function is to assist the small intestine for digestion and metabolism of fatty acids. The excess bile acids secreted by the liver are stored in the gallbladder for future fatty acid metabolism.

Recent trends in the American pediatric diet confirm a direct correlation between gallbladder disease and childhood obesity. If the gallbladder is dysfunctional, then the child will be passing undigested fatty acids through the small and large intestine further compounding the elimination of toxins from the body. Consult with a physician if you suspect upper right stomach quadrant pain, especially after your child eats a food source containing fatty acids.

An effective home remedy to cleanse the gallbladder:
one ounce of virgin olive oil mixed with one ounce of fresh squeezed whole lemon juice.

An effective home remedy to cleanse the kidney, liver and intestines:
squeeze one whole lemon into one cup of hot water 3x a week

These simple cleanses for positive digestive health involving the liver, kidney, gall bladder, stomach and intestines may be consumed under your doctor's supervision upon physical examination. The gut, small intestine, and large intestine are the most prevalent systems that become dysfunctional in child development due to poor nutrition and toxin exposure, which may negatively affect a healthy mind.

Development of leaky gut syndrome must be prevented to allow maximum absorption of nutrients into the bloodstream and eventually into the brain. Optimum intestinal toxin elimination is a prerequisite to good health. Parents will have to, at some point in their child's development, address gastrointestinal issues. Whether the condition involves chronic diarrhea, constipation, or generalized stomach pain, a child will have these symptoms.

The preservation of an optimal gut and intestinal flora is critical to the production of neurotransmitter precursors which are the building blocks for cognitive and emotional thought processes. The healthier the gut, the healthier the brain will become. An efficient Brain-Gut Connection epitomizes the development of a healthy mind. Reference Diagram D

Simply stated, the Brain-Gut Connection involves precise communication between the Central Nervous System (brain and spinal cord) and the Enteric Nervous System (nerve flow to the gastrointestinal tract, pancreas, stomach and gall bladder). Over 90 percent of the nerve messages that allow the stomach to function, originate from the Enteric Nervous System not the brain

The Enteric Nervous System, embedded in the lining of the gut, has its own supply of neurons and neurotransmitters responsible for communicating, remembering as well as learning. Additionally, over 75 percent of the body's immune cells, essential for immune responses, are produced in the stomach.

There are three gut barriers that protect the essential biological functions within the stomach as well as the small intestine. The mechanical barrier is comprised of neuron, endocrine and mucosal epithelial cells. The immune barrier comprised of immune cells acts like the blood-brain-barrier in the brain, providing an internal filtration system to remove toxins. The third barrier is called the ecological barrier which must provide an optimal bacterial flora to allow the gut to function.

If a normal gut and intestinal flora exists, then the precursors for optimal neurotransmitter production in the brain will occur. For example, tryptophan contained in turkey, chicken and egg whites is converted into

5-hydroxy-tryptophan in the small intestine. This compound is then transferred to the brain and converted to the neurotransmitter serotonin. If toxins accumulate in the gut and small intestine, then the supply of serotonin will become diminished and may produce behavioral symptoms, including cognitive function, focus, and emotional dysfunction over a period of time.

Stresses to the body may adversely affect the Brain-Gut Connection. When a child or young adult is under stress due to poor nutrition or toxin exposure, then the Central Nervous System signals the release of cortisol, which is the body's primary stress hormone. This hormone in severe cases may create leaky gut syndrome, irritable bowel disease as well as systemic disease. Therefore, it becomes critical to keep your family's mental health on a positive path by removing all sources contributing to stress and toxin exposure to the body.

There are good and bad stresses that cause cortisol release in the body. The good or healthy stresses involve setting achievement goals. Children and young adults should be encouraged to plan and achieve goals. Although cortisol may be released into the body during the planning stages of a goal, the body's cortisol level returns to normal once achievement is reached. Even if children do not reach their goals, teach them the value of planning and persevering.

On the other hand, bad stress, or distress involves the release of cortisol which accumulates in the body due to increased anxiety with no reflex mechanism to eliminate cortisol from the body. Bad lifestyle choices feed the cortisol accumulation cycle which is a contributing factor in the onset of childhood behavioral symptoms. Teenagers may become unaware that their actions over a short period of time actually lead to ADHD, anxiety and depressive behavioral conditions.

Cortisol has two important actions. Cortisol breaks down protein and fat into glucose in the liver. Essentially this hormone takes fatty acids from fat tissue, protein from muscle and increases glucose into the bloodstream. Secondly, it tries to activate the anti-inflammatory and anti-stress response in the body. Additionally, cortisol blocks the flow of glucose into tissue, other than the Central Nervous System. If the stress to the body is chronic and severe then cortisol may impair the natural function of the immune system. The following symptoms may occur as a result:

- Poor memory
- Increased insulin release leading to reactive hypoglycemia response
- Frequent urination
- Sour stomach
- Decreased cellular potassium leading to muscle cramping and fatigue
- Increased sodium retention
- Irritable behavior
- Irregular bowel movements

The body's response to cortisol accumulation may eventually cause severe bipolar symptoms. Therefore, the underlying cause of behavioral conditions including ADHD, anxiety, and depression, especially in the child and young adult population, may actually be acute medical conditions involving cortisol with very easily treatable options, not involving powerful ADHD stimulant and psychiatric medications.

Adrenaline is the "fight or flight" stress hormone immediately secreted by the adrenal glands after a signal from the brain senses your body is in an emergency situation. Cortisol is also a stress hormone secreted by the adrenal glands. However, the release is in minutes rather than adrenalin release in seconds. Cortisol is the stress hormone that may accumulate and is associated with behavioral challenges in children. The ultimate release of cortisol from the adrenal glands is precipitated by the pituitary gland in the brain to release adrenocorticotropic hormone (ACTH). Again, a simple lesson in human biochemistry should be explored prior to powerful ADHD and psychiatric medication in children.

So, how can parents, educators or healthcare professionals help children and young adults understand what the solution is to prevent cortisol from overtaking their life, possibly creating behavioral challenges?

- **Consistent exercise:** teach children at a very early age the importance of regular physical exercise. Get them involved in school sports or activities that involve cardiovascular exercise for 30 minutes a day. This activity builds confidence and self-esteem. If school activity is not possible encourage exercise at home or the local gym. Exercise, especially aerobic, is scientifically proven to reduce cortisol accumulation.

- **Laughter and lightheartedness:** Teach children and young adults the importance to remain calm in stressful situations. Try to laugh as much as possible with your family and friends. Laughter is also scientifically proven to reduce cortisol levels.

- **Develop social networking relationships:** The opposite of social networking or connectivity is isolation. Isolation, especially in the young child population, may have an effect of raising cortisol stress hormones during a short period of time leading to the onset of behavioral symptoms including aggression. Encourage children at an early age to "get involved" and make new friends. The human mind is wired for social networking to promote positive mental health.

- **Meditation:** Meditation in the form of yoga or guided visualization may prove to be very relaxing for children and young adults who experience behavioral challenges. Their body and mind need to come into balance and remove stress hormones, including cortisol. A 15 minute meditation session may become the best medicine to effectively lower your blood pressure, decrease heart rate and most importantly reduce cortisol accumulation.

The behavioral question is...do we as parents, educators and healthcare professionals overlook the effects of cortisol accumulation as well as the Brain-Gut Connection? Or should we have more concern as to the etiology or cause of gastric and intestinal dysfunction if the child presents a chronic ADHD or psychiatric behavioral condition? One of the possible causes of chronic gastric and intestinal distress in children and adults is undiagnosed parasitic infection.

Diagram D
THE BRAIN-GUT CONNECTION

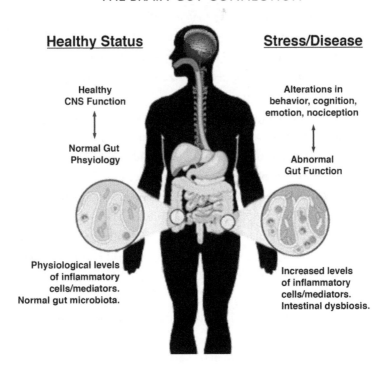

Healthy Status

Healthy
CNS Function

↑↓

Normal Gut
Phsyiology

Physiological levels
of inflammatory
cells/mediators.
Normal gut microbiota.

Stress/Disease

Alterations in
behavior, cognition,
emotion, nociception

↑↓

Abnormal
Gut Function

Increased levels
of inflammatory
cells/mediators.
Intestinal dysbiosis.

Dr. Frank Nova, chief of Parasitic Diseases at the National Institute of Health Laboratory, states, "In terms of numbers, there are more parasitic infections acquired in the United States than in Africa." Dr. Hazel Parcells, a parasite expert, believes that "eighty-five percent of Americans are infected with parasites".[36] The two most common types of intestinal parasites are protozoa and helminths.

Giardia lamblia is the most commonly transmitted protozoan parasite infection in humans. This parasite reproduces primarily in the small intestine causing giardiasis and does not circulate into the bloodstream. According to the Center for Disease Control, Giardia is the most common form of waterborne disease. Giardiasis is not entirely eradicated by chlorinated treatment facilities in the United States. Additionally, this protozoan is the primary parasite infecting dogs, cats, cows, and deer. Therefore, it is important to have children wash their hands after handling pets and washing fruits and vegetables thoroughly before eating. Other less prevalent protozoa parasites include cryptosporidium and entamoeba organisms.

Helminths are parasitic worms of which four classes currently exist, including trematodes (flukes), monogeneans, cestodes (tapeworm), and the nematodes (roundworms). The World Health Organization (WHO) estimates that 3.5 billion people worldwide are infected with some form of helminth infection masked as other chronic illnesses. WHO also classifies parasitic infections as the sixth most dangerous disease to infect the human body. Furthermore, the Center for Disease Control and Prevention estimates that over sixty million people in the United States are likely to be infected with Toxoplasma gondii, a parasite found in raw meat and cat feces.

As parasitic infections develop in their active cycles by feeding on the human host, parasitic symptoms mimic chronic diseases if not correctly diagnosed. These chronic illnesses include irritable bowel syndrome (IBS), gastroesophageal reflux disease, colitis, eczema, anemia, chronic fatigue syndrome, and allergies.

Additionally, the undiagnosed roundworm ascariasis is directly linked to the onset of lactose- intolerance allergic conditions. If the long-term misdiagnosis continues, the ascariasis parasite may be transported into lung tissue leading to the onset of asthmatic conditions in children.

The unpopular helminth infecting many children in the summertime is the fluke parasite called schistosomiasis. This parasite is directly responsible for "swimmer's itch" attacking the body while swimming in shallow inland lakes. Typically, the schistosomiasis parasite will not invade the body. However, if severe itching occurs, wash the entire body with antibacterial soap and towel dry the body. Topical hydrocortisone may be required in certain areas of the skin that exhibit extreme itchiness. Essentially, swimmer's itch is primarily a topical parasitic infection with limited internal causation of illness.

Ringworm or dermatophytosis is not to be misconstrued as a parasitic infection. Ringworm is caused by an overgrowth of yeast or fungi, topically. This common topical infection in children is most effectively treated with over the counter clotrimazole cream, zinc oxide paste, and a thin layer of one percent hydrocortisone cream.

Many malabsorption and nutritional deficiencies are evident with parasitic infections. As a parasitic infection spreads undiagnosed over time, protein, iron, and enzyme deficiencies can be directly related to decreased cognitive function and intellectual development of a child's healthy mind. Eventually, the child's immunity for fighting infection is compromised leading to secondary infections and other chronic illnesses due to excessive toxins trapped in the body.

Once the links between helminth infections and various forms of malnutrition are established, there are a number of pathways by which parasite burden may affect cognitive behavior. For example, poor performance on normal growth indicators appears to be correlated with lower school achievement and enrollment, worse results on some forms of testing, and a decreased ability to focus; on the other hand, iron deficiency may result in mild growth reduction, difficulty with abstract cognitive tasks, and lower scores on tests of mental and motor development . . . as well as increased fearfulness, inattentiveness, and decreased social responsiveness among very young children.[37] Anemia has also been associated with reduced stamina for physical labor, a decline in the ability to learn new information, and apathy, irritability, and fatigue according to the World Health Organization.[38]

Children under the age of five and teenagers may become susceptible to parasitic infections for different reasons. Children under the age of five always have their hands, foreign objects, and dirt going into their mouth. Teenagers on the other hand are the connoisseurs of fast food, which is more prone to parasitic infestation than a home-cooked whole-foods diet.

Mosquito bites, restaurant foods, and the water supply are sources for possible parasitic infections. Parasite infections with symptoms overlooked by parents and physicians may include

- digestive disorders
- irritability
- anal itching

- hyperactive behavior
- ADHD symptoms
- skin rashes
- acne
- poor memory
- fatigue
- chronic allergies
- deficient concentration
- sleeplessness
- menstrual abnormalities in teenagers

Parasitic infections exhibit similar symptoms as other chronic illnesses. Parents and physicians should agree to conduct multiple testing for parasitic infections prior to medicating children for a secondary behavioral diagnosis. Once again the term differential diagnosis is critical to implement the most appropriate treatment for the causation of a child's symptoms. Parents should also realize that most parasites may burrow into the lining of the small and large intestine and go undetected in stool sample assays.

Hook worm: one of the most prevalent and undiagnosed diseases in the United States afflicting over one billion people worldwide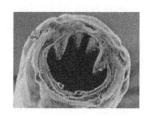

In children and young adults, undiagnosed hookworm infection may cause behavioral symptoms, and in severe undiagnosed cases may lead to retardation.

The hookworm larvae may penetrate the skin and find its way to the small intestine. Once attached to the small and large intestine, they feed on your blood supply while blocking nutritional absorption of food. During a short period of time, damage to the intestinal mucosa occurs.

The maximum length of hookworm growth is 1/2 inch.

Due to extensive iron loss in the blood, decrease mental acuity, appetite and even cardiac function may become likely consequences to untreated hookworm as well as any parasitic infection.

Dogs can be primary carriers of the hookworm. Be proactive with your family pet's health as well as your digestive health.

NATURAL PARASITIC CLEANSE:

If you or a family member suspects parasitic infection, seek medical assessment. While waiting for results, the following natural ingredients found at your local health food store will help eliminate parasites. The purpose of using these ingredients in your everyday diet helps:

- Kill parasites and their eggs
- Repair the small intestinal tissue lining
- Increase intestinal absorption of nutrients
- Eliminates toxins from the body
- Most importantly.....increase energy

TUMERIC POWDER:

Tumeric powder spice is a high antioxidant and immune system enhancer. Most importantly, turmeric spice possesses antiseptic properties in the human body and is a very good cleansing agent to eradicate yeast as well as parasitic infections. Tumeric is a member of the ginger family of spices, and exhibits a yellow color used in many Indian food dishes.

Additionally, research recommends turmeric spice incorporated into the family diet to support brain health as well as decrease hardening of the arteries. Tumeric has shown to be effective in reducing platelet aggregation which is the primary cause of arteriosclerosis.

A diet that consistently uses turmeric will help the body digest fats and sugars, thereby decreasing cholesterol from forming gallstones. There are many food dishes that taste very good with turmeric. However, I recommend turmeric in the form of a tea to achieve maximum therapeutic benefits for the elimination of parasitic as well as yeast infections.

GARLIC:

Garlic strengthens immune system function as well as an anti-parasitic agent. Once ingested into the body, garlic may paralyze parasites as well as other infectious organisms including yeast, bacteria and viruses. Garlic may also improve circulation and reduce cholesterol and blood pressure.

CLOVE OIL:

Many parasites burrow into the intestinal wall and lay their eggs. Pain is associated when parasites hatch the eggs. Clove oil can help mitigate the pain as well as kill the parasitic eggs. Clove powder and clove oil is a very good anti-parasitic, antibacterial as well as antiseptic agent. Researchers revere clove oil as the best spice to kill parasitic eggs. This spice also is very effective in stimulating digestive elimination and has positive effects against intestinal ulcerations.

BLACK WALNUT:

The black walnut tree is one of the most medicinally therapeutic trees in the United States. The tree bark, husk, shell and the actual kernel, in combination, help rid the body of parasites. The black walnut kernel is a very potent blood oxygenator which is the primary mode of parasite elimination. Additionally, this kernel has an abundance of omega-3 fatty acids and iodine. The iodine acts as an antiseptic attaching to the parasites and eventually causing death to the organisim.

Parasitic infections exhibit similar symptoms as other chronic illnesses. Parents and physicians should agree to conduct multiple differential testing for parasitic infections prior to medicating children for a secondary behavioral diagnosis. Once again the term differential diagnosis is critical to implement the most appropriate treatment for the causation of a child's symptoms. Parents should also realize that most parasites may burrow into the lining of the small and large intestine and go undetected in stool sample assays.

Bio-energy feedback scanning as well as a blood and stool assay is recommended for most accurate results. Since parasitic symptoms are now realized, effective and thorough treatment is extremely important. Consult with a specialist in parasitology as well as a gastroenterologist for appropriate monitoring if you feel your child has severe gastrointestinal symptoms.

The following dietary and supplementation interventions for children and young adults should be incorporated daily to maintain positive digestive health.

1. **Hydration** is critical to optimize digestive health by filtering the kidneys and removing water-soluble toxins from the body. Purified water sources are essential. Teenagers and adults require one to two liters a day depending on exercise and activity. Distilled or reverse osmosis water purification is considered a good source. Additionally, make a fresh hot lemon tea three times a week to cleanse the kidney, liver and urinary bladder by adding lemon juice from a fresh whole lemon squeezed into hot purified water.

2. **Fiber** intake is critical to optimize digestive health by cleansing toxic fecal plaques in the small and large intestinal wall. Countries in other parts of the world recommend 70–80 grams of fiber a day. The recommended daily allowance (RDA) in the United States is only twenty-five grams a day, which is not adequate. Children and young adults should consume at least fifty grams of fiber a day to ensure effective elimination of toxins, and fecal plaque adhering to the intestinal lining.

Natural psyllium husk is most preferred, in granular form, without chemical additives including aspartame, silicon dioxide, FD&C yellow #6, aluminum lake, as well as natural and artificial flavorings. The question and concern to manufacturers, who incorporate these toxic chemicals with psyllium husk, is why contaminate a product that is beneficial to the human body in its natural form without chemical additives and toxins?

Take psyllium husk after one hour of adequate water intake. Mix one tablespoon in eight ounces of water once a day. Do not take with food as psyllium will decrease absorption of food enzymes during the digestive process. Psyllium granules mixed in water is most effective to increase colonic and intestinal peristalsis, which eliminates chronic constipation leading to the possibility of irritable bowel syndrome. Make a smoothie for your child to mask the gritty texture. Remember that gritty psyllium husk is what will clean and detoxify the colon. Do not consume sugar-free psyllium as this product contains aspartame, which may cause neurotoxic side effects. Adults should consume at least sixty grams of fiber daily as studies show that a seven to ten percent reduction in low-density lipoprotein (LDL) or bad cholesterol is possible with increased daily fiber intake.

3. **Garlic** intake is an important consideration in optimizing digestive health by increasing immunity to disease. Consuming raw garlic or 1,000 mg concentrated odorless tablets daily creates increased hydrogen sulfide circulation in the bloodstream providing potent antioxidant properties as well as paralyzing and destroying any parasitic growth within the digestive tract. The odorless tablet or capsule form absorbs into the bloodstream from the small intestine thereby eliminating foul garlic odor.

4. **Vitamins, especially Vitamin D3, and minerals, including magnesium** are essential for the development of a healthy mind. Our food sources have been depleted of essential vitamins and minerals due to decades of soil erosion. Minerals are necessary for the production of enzymes, which in turn are required for the production of neurotransmitters. Vitamins, especially in children and teenagers at a recommended daily allowance are necessary to help the body prevent the accumulation of free radical oxidants in the body.

5. **Probiotic** supplementation, including Probacillus manufactured by www.ProJobaKids.com is necessary to restore normal bacterial flora in the large intestine if a child has a parasite infection. The probiotic, Lactobacillus, is effectively used in babies as an adjunct treatment for rotavirus. The two most common productive probiotics are Lactobacillus and Bifidobacterium. Lactobacillus bulgaricus helps relieve symptoms of lactose intolerance by attacking harmful bacteria that accumulates or adheres to the gastric and intestinal lining. The toxins released by harmful bacteria are also minimized or destroyed by probiotics, which produce essential B vitamins that aid in the appropriate digestion of food, thereby reducing the propensity for anemia.

6. **Sleep** must not be underestimated by children and adolescents. The recommended amount of uninterrupted sleep is between seven and eight hours per night. Adequate sleep, especially in the form of rapid eye movement, helps the body heal and repair cellular oxidative damage

that occurs during the day. This cellular oxidation is primarily due to the exposure of environmental toxins we endure on a daily basis.

These six elements of optimizing digestive health are essential in the development of a child's healthy mind. Effective elimination of toxins from the body while producing an abundance of cellular antioxidants helps optimize a child's psychoneuroendocrine function. Through appropriate supplementation and nutrition, a child presenting behavioral symptoms may revert to normal behavior prior to the implementation of drug therapy. Toxins trapped in the body may, during the course of time, alter the hormonal or biochemical balance required to maintain a healthy mind. Therefore, as parents, make healthy nutritional interventions to ensure our child achieves positive behavioral development.

Other considerations in the achievement of a healthy mind involve physical exercise. Physical exercise increases blood flow and oxygen to the brain. Aerobic exercising, in particular, increases brain-derived neurotrophic factor (BDNF) protein secretion in the brain, which multiplies the connections between neurons. This multiplication of neuronal connections produces increased psychoneuroendocrine function, which may lead to greater cognitive development. BDNF is a member of the neurotrophin growth factors, which are related to nerve growth factors. In severely depressed patients, BDNF blood plasma levels may decline as much as threefold. Furthermore, BDNF is reduced in patients with epilepsy.[39]

Exercise is an important factor in the development of a healthy mind by increasing the concentration of BDNF . Additionally, multiple endorphins are released by the pituitary and hypothalamus gland during exercise. Endorphins are naturally produced protein opioid peptides, which function as neurotransmitters. However, a child presented with a past closed head injury causing a permanent epileptic condition may have an increased incidence to develop depression.

Closed head injuries in many cases cause a significant and permanent decrease in BDNF not reversible by the benefits of exercise. Therefore, a child with a closed head injury accident must be thoroughly evaluated by a neurologist with many years of head trauma experience. Appropriate and immediate assessment is critical to rule out physiological as well as biochemical long-term damage due to brain trauma.

Many considerations are involved in developing a healthy mind. The nutritional, environmental, and physiological factors in this discussion should be assessed on a yearly basis with your child's physician. As a child develops and experiences new challenges in life, assessment of their overall health is essential. If symptoms of a behavioral condition arise, parents now have acquired knowledge to discuss with their physician and rule out underlying cause or etiology of the child's behavioral condition. Parents should constructively engage with their child's physician or therapist to obtain the most effective and prudent treatment plan for behavioral conditions, thereby promoting the development of a healthy mind.

Notes

_____

_____

_____

_____

_____

_____

_____

_____

_____

_____

_____

_____

_____

_____

_____

_____

_____

_____

_____

_____

_____

Ask the Pharmacist • www.CAOOY.org

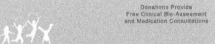

Helping Determine Causation
of Behavioral Conditions

Donations Provide
Free Clinical Bio-Assesment
and Medication Consultations

CAOOY

Coalition Against Overmedicating Our Youth

WORLD   ADVOCATE   FOR   CHILDREN©

CHAPTER 9

Psychological and Alternative Bio-assessments

With respect to children, stimulant and psychiatric medications represent two of the most powerful pharmacological drug classes prescribed in the practice of American pediatric medicine. Stimulant drug therapy in the form of synthetic amphetamine compounds may effectively increase a child's dopamine, norepinephrine, or serotonin neurotransmitter function, providing improved cognitive function and behavioral development, in a short period of time.

Psychiatric medications including antidepressants, mood stabilizers, anti-anxiety and anti- psychotic drugs may provide effective immediate control of behavioral symptoms that require crisis management of high-acuity psychiatric patients in the hospital environment as well as in community practice.

However, the probable long-term side effects of these two pharmacological drug classes in children signal a concern to consider alternative assessment and treatment plans prior to premature drug therapy. Prudent use of these medications must be mandated for use in children.

Children currently taking these medications should not immediately discontinue their course of therapy.

Consult with a physician specializing in psychiatric medication reduction therapy if a gradual discontinuation of drug treatment is desired. Upon consulting with a physician, discontinuation or reduction in drug therapy is recommended in accordance with the Action Plan for Childhood Behavioral Conditions.

Many psychiatrists as well as physicians in other medical disciplines are now realizing that alternative assessment and treatment plans, in conjunction with less drug therapy, presents a more safe and effective modality to help children regain normal behavior.

Alternative assessments provide options for parents and physicians to consider, prior to medication therapy. Psychiatrists practicing prudent use of medication in children should recommend the Informed Consent Document for ADHD and Psychiatric Medications to their governing body. This adoption will create a more effective dialog between the physician and parent in determining alternative treatment plans prior to prematurely prescribing stimulant and psychiatric medications.

Alternative treatment plans in conjunction with medication therapy may reduce the frequency and dosage of powerful stimulant and psychiatric drugs, while providing a more therapeutic outcome with fewer side effects in the child's treatment plan. During the last fifteen years, children in America have developed chronic illnesses normally exhibited by adults. These illnesses include cardiac disease, diabetes, and chronic asthma.

Furthermore, ADHD, autism, and psychiatric conditions in children are reaching epidemic rates. As a society, we must ask why? Striving for answers, exploring all options for parents, and exploring all options relevant to causation of a child's behavioral condition should be the new focus.

Bio-energy feedback studies reveal that "two thirds of all illnesses are caused by toxins in the body, while only one third is due to genetics and trauma to the body." In other words, sixty-seven percent of childhood behavioral symptoms involving ADHD and psychiatric conditions should begin with a toxicology bio-assessment to rule out causation. Bio-energy feedback scanning may provide critical information during the initial bio-assessment of children with behavioral symptoms.

Bio-energy feedback is not a treatment, diagnosis, or cure for illness. However, the results produced by bio-energy feedback scanning provide physicians, parents, and educators an initial course of action to treat children exhibiting behavioral disorders. Bio-energy feedback scanning involves the detection of possible disruption of energy flow that our bodies signal when under stress due to disease, toxins, or trauma. The scanning process is quick and noninvasive, lasting approximately twenty-five minutes. Children comply very well to the procedure.

According to acclaimed Belgian biochemist Ilya Prigogine, recipient of the 1977 Nobel Peace Prize in chemistry, "blocked energy flow throughout the body can eventually manifest as illness. At first, these blockages demonstrate tiredness, fatigue, and muscular pain. Later, chronic illness appears".[40]

Since the late 1970s, technological advances in bio-energy feedback scanning have grown tremendously. The ability to identify blocked energy flow "signatures" depicts precise markers of the body that are under stress or toxic exposure. If the mind and body are in a healthy state, elimination of toxins including metabolic waste toxins from the digestive process is possible. The body will bring itself back to homeostasis or stable condition. This process is also considered homotoxicology, wherein the body reacts to chemical toxins or stresses from the environment, poor digestion, or poor elimination. There are six phases of homotoxicology involving the process of effectively or ineffectively eliminating toxins or stresses from the body. Parents should be aware that this process begins at the birth of your child.

1. **Phase one:** Begins with elimination by the body. In response to toxin or stress to the body, a child will try and expel the toxin through sneezing, vomiting, sweating, coughing, or excretion via the urine or feces. If the child is not successful during this process, then the body proceeds to phase two.

2. **Phase two:** Begins a reactive process to the trapped toxin or stress through an inflammatory process. Mucus production, swelling, and fever

attempts to move the toxin to phase one for elimination. If unsuccessful, the body response moves to phase three.

3. **Phase three:** Begins by depositing the toxin in a specific area of the body. This response naturally occurs until the body can obtain the elimination capability to remove the toxin through phase two. If this response is not successful, the body response moves to phase four. Parents with a child exhibiting a behavioral condition should understand the importance of phase three. Toxins may contribute to the causation of behavioral symptoms. Premature drug therapy without identifying toxins may exacerbate the condition later in life by developing secondary behavioral symptoms related to undiagnosed toxin accumulation.

4. **Phase four:** Begins with the accumulation of toxins within a specific area of the body eventually creating a dysfunctional system. For example, toxins or stresses may extensively accumulate in the large intestine. This will create a breakdown in the elimination process of the large intestine. Over a period of time, the body may develop chronic illness including irritable bowel syndrome, colonic polyps, diverticulitis, or colitis. If not resolved, the body moves to phase five.

5. **Phase five:** Begins the degenerative process. The body becomes dysfunctional with chronic illness. Many chronic illnesses exist due to the progression toward phase five. These chronic diseases may include lupus, fibromyalgia, multiple sclerosis, and end-stage cardiac failure. Many patients may move through phase five escaping major complications and merely exhibit chronic fatigue. Their condition may worsen and lead to phase six. However, many patients die prior to entering the last phase.

6. **Phase six:** This phase represents the body yielding to significant degeneration of organ systems. Many malignant cancers represent this phase. The expression of oncogenes causes mutation within the cellular structure causing irreversible growth in cells that should normally die. This phase represents eventual death of the body.[41]

Parents must be given the opportunity to discuss with their child's physician, via informed consent, alternative assessments, as well as treatments prior to prematurely prescribing stimulant and psychiatric medications. The decision to medicate a child can be a very emotional consideration as a parent weighs the positives and negatives of drug therapy. Comprehensive assessments via differential diagnosis are critical in a parent's decision making. With alternative assessments like bio-energy feedback scanning, parents have more data regarding their child's heath status to make an informed decision.

A concerned parent contacted me regarding her fourteen-year-old daughter's diagnosis of inattentive ADD. Her daughter gradually lost focus and motivation. Her days were filled with forgetfulness, lack of energy, and poor appetite. During our discussion, she mentioned that the only significant medical history for her daughter involved a one-week extra stay in the hospital due to a violent vaccine reaction after birth. Upon close observation after birth, her daughter was finally released a week later. The mother stated that her daughter had a normal childhood until her inattentive attention deficit diagnosis six months previous to her fourteenth birthday. The stimulant therapy over a period of three months was slightly effective, and she had reservations about maintaining her daughter on stimulant drug therapy without any answers as to causation of her behavior.

Due to her daughter's vaccine reaction at birth, I suggested a heavy metal toxicity screen via bio-energy feedback. The bio-assessment was positive for heavy metal toxin. After successful chelation therapy, as well as nutritional intervention, her daughter reverted to normal behavior.

Some traditional "medical science" physicians view the "natural science" of homotoxicology as a nontraditional assessment in a child with behavioral symptoms. However, physicians are becoming more open to alternative testing and treatment in conjunction with the traditional testing protocols. The end result is that children faced with behavioral conditions have more options to help revert to normal behavior. As a parent with six children, I would rather have options for alternative and traditional assessments to help reverse my child's behavioral condition.

There are many great physicians in America with high ethical standards of practice. They go above and beyond traditional protocols established by their respective disciplines of medical practice. They have true concern for the long-term well-being of their patients. They go above protocol to ensure that patients receive positive outcomes.

America's ADHD epidemic in children can be resolved by returning to this standard of practice . . . a practice wherein causation of behavioral symptoms are identified, prior to immediate drug therapy, and a mandate by the DEA to enforce a more strict policy in prescribing stimulant as well as psychiatric drug therapy in children. Parents of a child currently taking stimulant therapy should request their doctor to appropriately monitor side effect response to therapy. Simply handing over a prescription without monthly comprehensive cardiac monitoring protocols as recommended in the Action Plan for Childhood Behavioral Conditions is not advisable.

Bio-energy feedback provides additional insight as to causation, while providing an alternative treatment plan depending on the results of all diagnostic assessments, both traditional as well as nontraditional. Bio-energy feedback scanning assesses over five thousand energy flow signatures in over seventy categories including but limited to the following:

- Pollens
- Molds/fungus
- Trees
- Parasites
- Pesticides
- Metals
- Herbs
- Bacteria
- Viruses
- Grasses
- Enzymes

As a child undergoes "traditional" assessment for ADHD, your doctor should be made aware that you are seeking "alternative" assessment from a psychotherapist who specializes in creative visualization, Response Inhibition, as well as multiple forms of Cognitive Behavioral Therapy including Rational Emotive Behavior Therapy. The therapist you select should have extensive training in these sciences as well as credible references.

The techniques taught to a child by a psychotherapist can promote coping mechanisms for their condition while a physician conducts a comprehensive differential diagnosis to determine a possible medical condition is the cause of symptoms.

Psychotherapy objectively tries to help the child realize their sense of well-being. Techniques utilized by a trained psychotherapist can help a child cope with stressful ADHD symptoms, including inattentive ADD and ADHD.

Creative visualization or guided imagery can help a child visualize, through a relaxed creative technique, the release of compounded environmental stresses. These stresses may involve issues at school or at home, not recognized by the parent until the compounded stresses manifest into an ADHD condition. Guided imagery may help a child by mentally meditating toward positive, happy imaginary images. In doing so, the positive feelings produced are transmitted to the brain.

Promptness in school homework, focused positive attitude, and positive attention may return to normal with these practiced techniques. These techniques may involve creating a space on a wall in your child's room that has pictures or mementos of things or places that they would like to visit one day, places, or pictures that make them happy.

A psychotherapist will help the child mentally visualize these exciting or happy places to visit. This process creates a sense of well-being and what is important within the mind. Once this sense of happiness is practiced over and over, the child will begin to develop a more positive attitude, while releasing stress. This positive attitude strengthened within the emotive thought process in the brain will eventually allow the child to focus on related schoolwork and deadlines. This phase of visualization is called focus-guided imagery, which teaches the child to mentally visualize tasks requiring completion.

Creative visualization and guided imagery are practiced by many Olympic and elite athletes around the world. In every sport, mental toughness is always stated when referring to a successful athlete. Mental toughness in elite athletes is not realized overnight. Just as an athlete will physically practice his or her sport, they will devote time and energy for focus- guided imagery training of the mind. This focus becomes a part of their daily routine.

A psychotherapist with experience in focus-guided imagery may be very helpful in training your child to increase their mental capacity and toughness. As a child proceeds through the initial ADHD or psychiatric assessment by their physician, focus-guided imagery helps provide mental coping skills. Renowned psychotherapists across America specialize in focus-guided imagery techniques. Over the years, teaching these techniques has helped many children, especially teenagers overcome their emotional behaviors. After successful intervention in teenage behavioral conditions, the Clarkston News in Clarkston, Michigan asked the important questions that are helping children win the battle against behavioral challenges. The question and answer dialog includes the following:

CN: What is guided imagery?

Therapist: Guided imagery is gentile yet powerful. Through the use of CDs and therapy, guided imagery can reach places inside the mind that conscious thinking sometimes cannot. It is proven to speed up healing, shown to reduce anxiety, pain, and fatigue. It may eliminate depression and improve self-esteem. Guided imagery can improve energy levels and increase healing by allowing the body and mind to relax and recharge.

CN: What is the subconscious mind?

Therapist: The subconscious mind is the blueprint of all our beliefs. These beliefs are derived from our past experiences. They come from parents, environment, and experiences of our life. The objective of hypnotherapy is to rid our mind of poor beliefs and replace them with empowering beliefs. The goal, especially in children with behavioral conditions, is to have the conscious and subconscious mind have the same empowering beliefs. The unconscious mind is located in the subconscious and has control of the immune system, autonomic bodily functions, as well as life experiences. Thoughts become actions. So it is very important that the thoughts originating from the subconscious mind are accurate, rational, valuable, true, and empowering. (Courtesy of the Clarkston News)

Another form of successful alternative treatment in ADHD is Response Inhibition (RI). RI involves the body's ability to control impulsive behavior, prioritizing behavior and setting goals. Resisting temptation is synonymous with RI. Resisting temptation and avoiding careless mistakes with schoolwork are common characteristics that become deficits in children exhibiting ADHD. Many behavioral studies show that impairment of neuro-motor transmission for the RI control center in the prefrontal cortex of the brain may be a causative factor in the ADHD condition.

The neurological deficiency in RI may be mitigated with the help of a psychotherapist. Techniques are available to a child for increasing prioritization, limiting impulsive behavior, as well as setting goals. Addressing RI is very important as a child enters their teenage years faced with a multitude of temptations due to peer pressure. Building self-esteem and self- confidence in a child is critical to optimizing RI.

A child's self-esteem or confidence cannot develop without the establishment of responsibilities. Enforcing responsibilities early in childhood behavioral development teaches self-worth. By age five, encourage your child to be responsible for jobs around the house that interest them. For example, allow them to set the dinner table every day and clean their bedroom. As they progress into peer-pressured teenage years, increase their responsibilities inside and outside of the family unit. Community service requirements are now mandatory in most high schools. Stress the importance of helping others less fortunate.

Also there is the ultimate sense of accomplishment at age sixteen. Teach your child goal orientation during the process of obtaining their driver's license. While attending driver's training classes, stress the importance of holding down a part-time job throughout high school. My children realize that a job is required prior to obtaining a driver's license. This teaches them the value of work ethic, while the focus on achieving a goal builds their self-confidence.

As your child approaches the teenage years, work with them on developing their maturity level. Discuss the value of remaining calm in various situations. Encourage communication through the expression of their emotions regarding sensitive topics in a calm manner without frustration. Many cases of inattentive ADHD in adolescent girls involve lack of emotion and response. Experienced psychotherapists can help a parent and child reach a happy medium and keep communication lines open. Communication with your child is essential during the process of reverting back to normal behavior.

CBT in many cases is used adjunctively to help mitigate psychiatric disorders as well as anxiety, substance abuse, and mood disorders. An experienced psychotherapist with good CBT credentials in REBT techniques may provide instrumental help for a child exhibiting a psychiatric behavioral condition.

Specifically, depression is the most common psychiatric behavioral condition in children. In America, 2.5 percent of children suffer from depression. Depression is most common in boys under the age of ten; however, by age sixteen, girls tend to have a far greater incidence.[42]

Parents should be aware the signs and symptoms of depression, including

- thoughts of worthlessness
- sleep pattern disruptions, excessive sleep, or sleeplessness
- anger
- lack of concentration
- chronic sadness

REBT, which is a specialized form of CBT, provides a cognitive approach for treatment of depression, anxiety, and stress. REBT addresses a child's irrational thought process and beliefs. Effective therapy through a multitude of REBT techniques helps a child replace irrational thoughts with more reasonable thoughts.

Psychotherapists, who teach REBT techniques, encourage a child to accept personal responsibility for their own thoughts, feelings, and behavior. Eventually, this type of therapy empowers their thought process and provides a positive belief system toward productive behavior. Within months, a child may experience new, positive ideas incorporated into their way of living.

PRINCIPLES OF RATIONAL EMOTIVE BEHAVIOR THERAPY

1. You are responsible for your actions.
2. Harmful emotions and dysfunctional behaviors are the aftereffects of your irrational thinking.
3. You can imbibe the realistic view in yourself and then practice them to make it your life's part.
4. You can experience more satisfactions in life by developing and following a reality-based perspective. By this you will tend to accept yourself more.

REBT distinguishes between practical problems and emotional problems. Practical problems are actual events and situations that are problematic, whereas emotional problems are reactions to such events that are inappropriate, inaccurate (over reactive or under reactive), and potentially harmful. While one cannot always control things that happen in life, one is responsible for what one makes of it and how one handles it.

REBT addresses the emotional suffering by the utilization of REBT techniques. Many techniques are employed by a trained psychotherapist. These REBT techniques include rational emotive imagery, in which children will imagine themselves thinking, feeling, and behaving in ways they would like to think, feel, and behave in real life. Role playing, desensitization, and assertiveness exercises also help a child obtain freedom from emotional upheaval and a more authentic and joyful engagement in life.

Without a child's emotional turmoil or addictions, the experience of involvement and joy becomes easier. Additionally, freedom to engage in gratifying experiences of spontaneity, commitment, and self-actualization becomes easier. REBT techniques may help a child take control of their life, instead of depending on a therapist for many years. Tools are given and practiced to identify and overcome causation of emotional difficulties. In a sense, the child eventually becomes their own therapist.

Enhancement of realistic beliefs will help a child eliminate present emotional and behavioral problems, while avoiding future ones. REBT is strengthened by the belief that how a child emotionally responds initially depends on their interpretations, views, beliefs, and thoughts of situations in life.[43]

The aforementioned principles of rational emotive behavior are paraphrased because these principles provide sensible solutions relevant to causation of many behavioral conditions facing our youth today, especially in the teenage population.

Developing and strengthening their emotional thought process is critical in combating the onset or the existence of behavioral conditions. In doing so, a child's addictions or inner turmoil may be effectively eliminated over a period of time. The selection of an experienced psychotherapist may help guide your child to recovery with the techniques and tools necessary to treat emotional pain and despair.

Notes

_____

_____

_____

_____

_____

_____

_____

_____

_____

_____

_____

_____

_____

_____

_____

_____

_____

_____

_____

_____

_____

_____

Ask the Pharmacist • www.CAOOY.org

CHAPTER 10

Leaders Must Lead

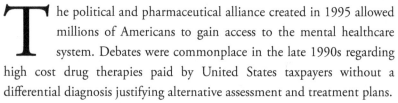

T he political and pharmaceutical alliance created in 1995 allowed millions of Americans to gain access to the mental healthcare system. Debates were commonplace in the late 1990s regarding high cost drug therapies paid by United States taxpayers without a differential diagnosis justifying alternative assessment and treatment plans.

During the past fifteen years, management and oversight authorities monitoring the foster care system, in particular, became ineffective to protect children in America. According to special investigators, namely prominent special investigator Allen Jones of Pennsylvania as well as the Government Accountability Office (GAO) Child Foster Care investigators....state mental health directors failed to monitor drug therapy guidelines for children.

As a former chief investigator for the Office of Inspector General, Bureau of Special Investigations, Mr. Jones rejected the intended purpose of the Texas Medication Algorithm Project (TMAP). In the mid to late 1990s, Mr. Jones warned of abuses involving excessive mental health drug therapy treatment. He recommended to his state leadership in Pennsylvania to reject the TMAP for the state of Pennsylvania. Due to his leadership role in protecting children, his recommendation to reject the TMAP forced his termination of employment. His role as a former investigator in the late 1990s predicted the behavioral health crisis afflicting today's youth in America.

Currently, Congressional leaders now realize that a mandate for reform regarding stimulant and psychiatric drug therapy in children is critical as a result of the Government Accountability Office Child Foster Care drug audit report in December 2011. America is missing a great opportunity to lead and compete in a global economic world due to the fact that we are divesting rather than investing in positive childhood behavioral development initiatives.

The statistical data contained within the GAO Child Foster Care drug audit, the plight of approximately 420,000 foster care children excessively overmedicated in America, is alarming for the future security and prosperity of our nation. Furthermore, over sixteen million children in America live in poverty, while one in four children under the age of five live in poverty.[44] This statistic represents additional contributing factors to the behavioral health crisis.

United States Senator, Thomas Carper, chairman of the Homeland Security and Government Affairs Committee, made a statement at the December 2011 meeting. He reacted to the GAO Child Foster Care report involving the overmedicating of our youth. "I was almost despondent to believe that the kids under age one, babies under the age of one, were receiving this kind of medication." From a pharmacist's perspective, there is no clinical rationale to prescribe psychoactive medications to a one-year-old child.

America is a nation of great leaders . . .

   . . . leaders in government

   . . . leaders in traditional and alternative medical care

   . . . leaders in education

   . . . leaders in community pharmacy practice

   . . . leaders in parenting, and

   . . . leaders of coalitions

Americans must unite and correct the injustices committed to our youth during the last forty years. The current state of government affairs lacks prudent, uniform state guidelines. Reform is required to reverse the premature prescribing of ADHD stimulant and psychiatric medications in our youth. The Action Plan for Childhood Behavioral Conditions provides bio-assessment recommendations as well as prudent prescribing guidelines for medicating our youth.

Senator Carper of Delaware, the primary requestor for the Government Accountability Office report should be commended....leading preliminary discussions, regarding the childhood behavioral health crisis, at the Senate Committee for Homeland Security and Government Affairs. The GAO Child Foster Care drug audit uncovered extensive mismanagement in the prescribing as well as the monitoring process of stimulant and psychiatric drug therapies given to foster and non-foster care children.

Investigative results by the GAO five-state drug audit prove to the American people that prudent drug-monitoring protocols as well as alternative assessments are required in the treatment of children with behavioral conditions. State Medicaid programs in the United States spend over six billion dollars annually on psychiatric drugs, which accounts for approximately 30 percent of the entire drug budget. This figure has doubled since 1999. Leaders in Congress, both democrats and republicans united, can effectively legislate an immediate solution to the behavioral health crisis afflicting children.

Specifically, a signed Informed Consent Document for ADHD and Psychiatric Medications by the physician and parent will ensure prudent use of drug therapy in children. Furthermore, informed consent would give parents options for effective alternative assessment as well as treatment plans prior to medicating children. These interventions may include Rational Emotive Behavior Therapy (REBT), focus-guided visualization and Response Inhibition (RI), as well as medical bio-assessments to rule out nutritional, physiological and environmental risk factors prior to premature drug therapy.

The Department of Health and Human Services in Washington DC, which oversees the Child Foster Care program, should take the initiative and demand uniform guidelines for all states. Accountability standards should reside with each state's mental health director, enforcing appropriate use of drug therapy in children. Prior to medicating our youth, the Department of Health and Human Services should mandate a differential diagnosis conducted by an independent physician to determine the causation of the behavioral condition. Currently, this policy is not mandated in community practice.

Unfortunately, many community psychiatrists across America are not practicing with the recommendation of differential diagnosing, nor are they informing the guardians of alternative bio-assessment and treatment plans including various forms of Cognitive Behavior Therapy. The deficiency to determine cause of behavioral conditions as disclosed in the GAO Child Foster Care report is an important contributing factor in the behavioral health crisis afflicting American children.

Upon review of the GAO Child Foster Care report, the Department of Health and Human Services (HHS) in Washington DC stated they would help states expand and strengthen their guidelines for the use of ADHD and psychiatric medications. If states were following laws regarding oversight provisions, the statement made by HHS would not be necessary. States are required by law to follow the Child and Family Services Improvement and Innovation Act as well as the Fostering Connections to Success and Increasing Adoptions Act to help protect children. Additionally, states should be required to follow the prudent monitoring protocols as recommended in the Action Plan for Childhood Behavioral Conditions.

Senator Carper has initiated the concern for reform in the medical assessment and treatment of children with behavioral conditions. He is a leader in government, as he brings this critical issue to the forefront of American politics, fearless of lobby influence. The Secretary of the United States Health and Human Services, which oversees the Child Foster Care program, is leading and is mandating all states in our union adhere to more strict guidelines as well as ensuring the prudent use of medications in children with behavioral conditions.

All state governments should recommend informed consent and differential diagnosing in community practice of psychiatry as a mandate in state mental health guidelines. Currently, these guidelines are not required, and contribute to the behavioral health crisis afflicting American children. The Department of Health and Human Services in Washington DC is actively correcting the injustices in psychiatric medical care for children. As one of the important leaders in government regarding this reform, Health and Human Services in Washington DC with an approximate annual budget of 900 billion dollars has the ultimate authority of ensuring initiated corrections are implemented by state mental health directors.

While writing this book, I received a response from the Department of Health and Human Services in Washington DC regarding my concerns of overmedicating our youth. The correspondence stated that "The Department of Health and Human Services is concerned about the safe, appropriate, and effective use of psychotropic medications among children. Recently, the Department provided State Directors with information outlining opportunities and ways they can strengthen their systems for prescribing and monitoring psychotropic medication use in children. An action plan addressing this issue is being developed by State Child Welfare Directors, Medicaid, and children's mental health agencies."

On April 29, 2013, Director of National Institute of Mental Health in Washington DC, Dr. Thomas Insel, stated that the system for assessing as well as treating patients with mental illness "lacks validity".......and patients "deserve better". This bold statement made by the director indicates a positive shift in the assessment and treatment process in children. He further stated that his agency is distancing itself from the antiquated Diagnostic and Statistical Manual for Mental Disorders. The National Institute of Mental Health in Washington is the largest mental health government agency with an approximate annual budget of 2 billion dollars overseeing mental health research.

However, in February 12, 2012, state of Michigan guidelines for prescribing ADHD stimulant drug therapy in children has not been revised. I received an e-mail from a foster parent of an eleven- year-old boy. She asked if her foster child would be able to receive brand name Adderall XR 20 mg at two capsules daily dosing, due to the national shortage of stimulant amphetamine medications used to treat ADHD. In a response e-mail, she stated that her son was able to receive the sixty capsules of Adderall XR 20 mg per month just as she was during the past two years paid by state Medicaid.

This long acting Adderall therapy is an adult dosage, beyond prudent prescribing recommendations for children. Furthermore, why is a taxpayer funded medication drug program still covering branded drug therapies? State mental health directors of Medicaid programs should re-evaluate the prescribing parameters for all amphetamine stimulant and psychiatric medications for children. Leaders in state government should mandate adherence for more complete prescribing guidelines as well as a mandatory generic drug formulary for drugs paid by the state Medicaid system.

Many physicians interviewed during the GAO Child Foster Care drug audit realize the importance of regulating and monitoring the use of powerful ADHD stimulant and psychiatric medications in children. Dr. Charles Zeenah, director of Child and Adolescent Psychiatry at Tulane University, states, "when you treat young children, you always try behavioral intervention before going to medication." Our leaders in state government should reach out to physicians, like Dr. Zeenah, who are proponents for the practice of prudent prescribing protocols in children with behavioral conditions.

These prudent prescribing protocols are starting to positively affect university instruction at prestigious institutions including Johns Hopkins University School of Medicine. Johns Hopkins University is a true institutional leader in reversing the negative trend regarding the practice of psychiatry during the last fifteen years. Dr. Margaret Chisolm, professor of Psychiatry at Johns Hopkins University School of Medicine, is one of the leaders, at her university and teaching hospital, making a positive impact on the direction of psychiatric practice for promising new physicians of psychiatry. Professors at Johns Hopkins University and teaching hospital lead by their actions, rather than following their psychiatric profession's misguided reverence to the Diagnostic and Statistical Manual of Mental Disorders.

The fifth edition of DSM was published and released in May 2013. Since the 1980s, the DSM has been governed by a few powerful psychiatrists. Effective leaders like Dr. Chisolm of Johns Hopkins University challenge those in power, especially when the safety and lives of children are at stake.

Dr. Chisolm, as well as many other physicians in America, lead the way for a new practice in psychiatry . . . a practice wherein psychiatrists consider the patient as an individual. In doing so, the psychiatrist may develop a personalized and systematic treatment plan while a medical doctor assesses underlying causation of symptoms due to nutritional, physiological, or environmental risk factors. Just as important, the psychiatrist is also the team leader while reviewing assessments made by highly qualified therapists for children with behavioral conditions.

In community practice, this team approach to treatment is imperative. A good psychiatrist evaluates the entire patient's assessments and eventually decides on the course of therapy, which may or may not involve drug therapy. Psychiatrists should be receptive in recommending alternative assessment and treatment plans prior to prematurely medicating children with behavioral symptoms. The aforementioned assessment process that I recommend school systems across America consider "promoting" to parents with children exhibiting behavioral symptoms is called the Action Plan for Childhood Behavioral Conditions.

Parents, educators, as well as all healthcare professionals have critical roles in the Action Plan for Childhood Behavioral Conditions.

Another factor that negatively affects the treatment of children with behavioral conditions involves state disability payments. Parents and foster parents are receiving significant monthly child disability checks from states for treatable child behavioral symptoms. Dr. Chisolm suggests in the Johns Hopkins Reflections on Clinical Excellence that the sharp rise in disability payments for treatable mood disorders is counterproductive in reverting patients back to normal psychological behavior. She states "I would add that disability payments can then make certain co-occurring illnesses such as substance abuse disorders more difficult to treat, creating even more disability."

The Department of Health and Human Services should mandate individual state inspectors conduct unannounced internal audits of child foster care homes. Furthermore, the reevaluation and reassessment of drug therapy for every foster care child in America should be a required guideline mandated by HSS. Many children in foster care are prescribed duplicate drug therapy as reported in the GAO Child Foster Care drug audit report. This reassessment will protect children while providing significant cost savings in state budgets due to the elimination of overmedicating our youth.

State budgets are constrained more than ever before in American history. Governors are trying to balance their budgets with less tax revenue from previous years while the costs of maintaining services escalate. In view of the GAO Child Foster Care report, uncovering excessive and inappropriate use of drug therapy in children, states could realize significant savings to their drug budgets by implementing more strict prescribing protocols for children with behavioral conditions.

A mandatory generic drug formulary for Medicaid and Medicare recipients would save the states from cutting their services. Stimulant and psychiatric drug therapy in children should be implemented only after a comprehensive differential diagnosis as well as Cognitive Behavior Therapy intervention. State governments should lead by enforcing prudent prescribing as well as monitoring guidelines for stimulant and psychiatric medications in children as recommended in the Action Plan for Childhood Behavioral Conditions.

The GAO Child Foster Care drug audit report also uncovered the use of powerful atypical antipsychotic drugs as chemical restraints in foster care children. Dr. George Fouras, a child psychiatrist and co-chairman of the Adoption and Foster Care Committee of the American Academy of Child and Adolescent Psychiatry (AACAP), states, "There is an incredible push to use medications to solve these problems as if it is a magic wand. We are trying to put a nice shiny term that sounds like 'oh we're just restraining the kid,' really what you are doing is just knocking them out to make them less of a problem for you". [44]

Dr. Fouras, along with many other psychiatrists across America, is speaking out for reform within their governing body.

- No longer can overmedicating practices against children continue
- No longer can leaders in government be silenced by lobbyists for the injustices toward children
- No longer can local, state, and federal policymakers ignore what is right for the protection of children
- No longer can billions of taxpayer dollars be squandered for inappropriate practices within the child foster care system.

Physicians, psychotherapists, parents, and educators have a unique opportunity to work together and solve the etiology or cause of childhood behavioral conditions prior to the implementation of drug therapy. During the past fifteen years, the current protocol according to the Diagnostic and Statistical Manual for Mental Disorders vastly supports drug therapy as the primary treatment intervention. Recently, however, the FDA now mandates that all stimulant and psychiatric drugs prescribed to children be given a federally approved Med Guide alert. All pharmacies that dispense these medications must comply with this new federal ruling.

The FDA Med Guide alert warns the public that stimulant and psychiatric medications pose a significant public health concern in children. Furthermore, the FDA Med Guide alert indirectly suggests that drug therapy not be implemented as primary treatment in children with behavioral conditions. The possible long-term risks are now apparent with the disclosure of the Med Guide alert mandated by the FDA.

The alternative assessment plans are not disclosed within the federally mandated Med Guide alert. However, The Action Plan for Childhood Behavioral Conditions has this disclosure. Physicians, psychotherapists, educators, and parents should work as a team to determine the alternative treatment plans prior to prematurely medicating children with powerful stimulant and psychiatric drug therapy.

Throughout the years, across America, there have been great leaders in our education system. Teachers and administrators in private as well as public school systems have implemented bold new programs helping children obtain higher levels of learning. The great leaders in education are invited to a bold new opportunity, and recommend the Action Plan for Childhood Behavioral Conditions.

Now is the time for the educational culture to change in a positive direction without overmedicating our youth. Teachers need to teach, administrators need to administrate, and children need to learn with the help of alternative assessment as well as treatment plans to reverse behavioral symptoms.

Education systems across America should adopt the team approach in the treatment of behavioral symptoms. This action plan assesses the cause of behavioral symptoms utilizing differential diagnosis to rule out nutritional, physiological, and environmental risk factors. The Action Plan for Childhood Behavioral Conditions immediately implements psychotherapy as well as comprehensive clinical bio-assessments.

Educators, parents, therapists, and physicians should agree that focused learning objectives are met by children with behavioral conditions. Alternative treatment plans should be implemented for children to meet learning objectives. Leaders in education should also realize that children with behavioral conditions have more to do with an underlying nutritional, physiological, or environmental causation rather than a parental shortfall. However, the home environment or family unit is a critical factor in the initial assessment of childhood behavioral conditions. Parents, educators, and therapists should understand that cause of symptoms is the most important consideration in helping children overcome their behavioral condition.

As the new protocols for medicating children begins the first phase of reform, national retail pharmacy chains should lead by enhanced counseling in children with stimulant and psychiatric drug therapy. In doing so, pharmacists will be recognized as expert medication advisors for the safe and effective use of stimulant and psychiatric medication therapy in children. Parents of children taking stimulant or psychiatric drug therapy should be aware of long- term side effects of these medications. Appropriate monitoring protocols should also be confirmed at the time of dispensing.

Pharmacists and physicians are encouraged to utilize The Action Plan for Childhood Behavioral Conditions as a reference source when counseling their patients. This reference will allow pharmacists as well as physicians to recommend supplementation, clinical bio-assessments as well as specific forms of psychotherapy for children not adequately controlled by medication. This reference will allow alternative treatment interventions rather than increased drug therapy to control symptoms until a causation of the behavioral condition is determined by a qualified medical doctor.

The system for medically treating children with behavioral conditions requires significant reform. For the past fifteen years, prudent prescribing and monitoring protocols in community practice are deficient. The recent GAO Child Foster Care drug audit report of December 2011 epitomizes the deficiencies in treating children with behavioral symptoms:

- ADHD and psychiatric behavioral conditions in children have reached epidemic rates
- Suicide rates in high schools across America are escalating
- Suicide is the second leading cause of death in the United States college student population.
- America's children consume three times the ADHD stimulant and psychiatric medications than the rest of the world's children combined.

As American citizens of our communities, leaders must act to protect, as well as appropriately treat, children with behavioral conditions. A team approach for treatment of behavioral symptoms is required to solve the overmedicating-our-youth epidemic. Specific reform that is encouraged involves implementation of the Action Plan for Childhood Behavioral Conditions. As previously discussed, this action plan will unite all treatment team disciplines toward the determining risk factors involved in the cause of childhood behavioral symptoms.

Leaders of coalitions and commissions provide many services to protect our youth. The Citizens Commission on Human Rights (CCHR) is the largest psychiatric watchdog organization in the world. With over four hundred chapters worldwide, this human rights organization has advocated a more strict enforcement of informed consent for the protection of mental health patients across the globe. CCHR advocates prudent prescribing and monitoring protocols, especially in the use of childhood behavioral conditions. They are not anti-psychiatry. They are ardent supporters of patient's rights in mental health. CCHR is directly responsible for helping to enact over 150 laws on safety issues related to mental health illness. Without their presence in the world as a patient advocate, the practice of psychiatry would be less regulated and more detrimental to the safety of children with mental illness.

The Coalition Against Overmedicating Our Youth is an organization whose mission is to implement the Action Plan for Childhood Behavioral Conditions. Their purpose is twofold...assist school districts as well as parents by reevaluating drug therapy regimens for children while recommending prudent drug protocols and alternative bio-assessment interventions. The drug regimens are assessed for prudent prescribing and monitoring protocols as well as a formal Drug Utilization Review. The Drug Utilization Review informs the parent and physician of possible immediate and long term drug to drug contraindications or harmful side effects of therapy.

After completion of a Drug Utilization Review, the Coalition Against Overmedicating Our Youth staff pharmacist initiates a recommendation summary to the parent, school administrator, physician, and therapist for review. The objective of the coalition is to increase alternative assessment interventions while recommending a gradual reduction in excessive stimulant and psychiatric drug therapy.

The GAO Child Foster Care report involved a two-year drug use audit in five geographically diverse states. The results were alarming. Foster care and non-foster care children were excessively medicated with ADHD stimulant and psychiatric medications. Differential diagnosing and alternative treatment plans were nonexistent. In many cases, foster children were placed in overcrowded foster parent homes. A team approach to therapy was not available.

After many years of reported abuses in the foster care system, Senator Carper requested the GAO audit. Since the alarming abuses became public knowledge in December 2011, leaders across America are voicing their outrage.

- The outrage that exploitation of overmedicating our youth could become a reality in American society.
- The outrage that over twelve million children and young adults in America may be unnecessarily medicated with ADHD stimulant and psychiatric medications.
- The outrage that America's children consume 3x the amount of ADHD and psychiatric drugs than the rest of the world's children combined.
- The outrage that suicide is the second leading cause of death in the college student population, possibly linked to long-term use of stimulant and psychiatric medications as a possible cause.

The Behavioral Health Crisis in America afflicting our children is here, festering day by day. Preservation of our next generation is the new mandate. American leaders must move forward and mandate reform of the current system that is

Over Medicating Our Youth

Notes

_____

_____

_____

_____

_____

_____

_____

_____

_____

_____

_____

_____

_____

_____

_____

_____

_____

_____

_____

_____

_____

Ask the Pharmacist • www.CAOOY.org

Helping Determine Causation
of Behavioral Conditions

Donations Provide
Free Clinical Bio-Assesment
and Medication Consultations

CAOOY

Coalition Against Overmedicating Our Youth

WORLD ADVOCATE FOR CHILDREN®

CHAPTER 11

A New Vision

Throughout history, American citizens have endured many
challenges and trials affecting the health of children. The health
crisis during the early 1990's involved the consumption of
tobacco products as well as the deliberate targeting and exploitation of the
child population by United States tobacco corporations.

Tobacco corporations were fully aware of the harmful effects in humans,
especially children. However, no package warnings were mandated by the
United States government. Prior to the 1990's, private litigation against the
tobacco industry involved eight hundred cases across the country. Not one
case was won by the people based on state consumer protection statutes,
negligent advertising and manufacturing practices.

Prior to 1994, outrage by the American people became more determined
and mobilized against the corporations for continuing to target harmful
products in children as well as adults. State attorney generals were pressured
by the people to act.

In 1994, Mississippi Attorney General, Mike Moore, filed the first
state litigation against the tobacco industry based on public health expenses
incurred in the treatment of tobacco induced disease. This case in Mississippi

involved the recovery of extensive Medicaid expenses due to antitrust law violations as well as the healthcare costs incurred by the state.

Attorney General Moore stated "This lawsuit is premised on a simple notion: you caused the health crisis: you pay for it." His dedication, through the will of people to do what was right for the health of children and adults, resulted in a landmark Tobacco Master Settlement Agreement. This settlement involved forty six states.

The Tobacco Master Settlement Agreement was a significant victory for people against a powerful established system which caused a child and adult health crisis under corporate control. These corporations included Phillip Morris USA, Lorillard Tobacco Company, Brown & Williamson Tobacco Corp, and R.J. Reynolds Tobacco Company. As a condition of settlement, these corporations were ordered to pay States 206 billion dollars over a twenty five year period.

There were many summary terms of this agreement important to the protection of children's health. The most important summary was the restriction of targeting, lobbying and advertising to the youth of our nation. These corporations had to establish, and pay for the National Public Education Foundation whose mission is to educate children on the dangers of smoking and the prevention of tobacco related diseases.

The United States tobacco corporations in the 1990's should have realized a greater societal benefit rather than targeting children's health and wellbeing for profit. Since the beginning of time, history has repeated itself in many aspects of human life. In today's America, history is repeating itself. Children are targeted by a different system.....a system that is medicating young children with powerful drugs prior to ruling out cause of their symptoms.

The challenge facing Americans today involves preserving the health and wellbeing of our next generation. Our children and young adults are victims that can no longer become trapped within a powerful system...a system that has created a behavioral health crisis afflicting our youth. For over twenty years parents and educators have been silenced by a powerful system of traditional medical treatment in children with behavioral conditions.

Traditional and alternative medicine should unite and silence the alarm:

- Over twelve million American children and young adults consume ADHD stimulant as well as psychiatric medications.
- America's children consume over three times the powerful stimulant and psychiatric medications than the rest of the world's children combined.
- Autism, ADHD, and opiate addiction has reached epidemic status
- GMO food production in America contains excessive herbicides including glyphosate, a powerfully toxic chemical causing behavioral health concerns
- Suicide is the second leading cause of death in the United States college student population.
- State Medicare/Medicaid stimulant and psychiatric drug expenditures have significantly increased to approximately forty percent of total annual drug budgets, forcing states to cut services.

State mental health directors have not enforced safe and effective drug prescribing as well as monitoring protocols, according to the United States Government Accountability Office Child Foster Care drug audit report of 2011. Landmark settlement cases, including the Johnson & Johnson litigation, validate a system of practice that requires reform.

The Secretary of the Department of Health and Human Services in Washington D.C. should mandate a strict guideline revision in the practice of child psychiatry, especially within the Child Foster Care Program. The two year United States Government Accountability Office audit of the Child Foster Care Program is an affirmation that the exploitation of a child's behavioral condition can no longer continue in America. The time has come for government leaders, elected by the people, mandate reform to the Diagnostic and Statistical Manual for Mental Disorders in children, and include a comprehensive assessment process....The Action Plan for Childhood Behavioral Conditions created by the Coalition Against Overmedicating Our Youth (CAOOY).

The traditional medication treatment plans can no longer continue as the primary intervention for children experiencing behavioral symptoms. Comprehensive bio-assessments to determine causation should become the new vision of treatment prior to prematurely medicating children with behavioral symptoms. Differential diagnosing prior to medicating children should be mandated by the Department of Health and Human Services. This system of treatment in childhood behavioral conditions should become the new vision of psychiatry.

American citizens should realize that the health and wellbeing of our next generation is in jeopardy. The behavioral health crisis involving children and young adults is reaching epidemic status. Suicide rates in the teenage and young adult population are escalating. The warning signs signal an alternate course of action.

Although ADHD stimulant drug therapy in children may provide effective short term resolution of symptoms in various forms of Attention Deficit Disorder, the FDA now mandates a Med Guide alert for all dispensed stimulant and psychiatric medications due to the known long term side effects. This action by the FDA is a direct response to the thousands of adverse drug reactions recorded by the FDA call center. The FDA Med Guide alert is defined as a class of drugs that pose a serious and significant public health consequence due to increased risk factors.

The Department of Health and Human Services which oversees the FDA should mandate a stricter guideline for bio-assessments, prior to medicating children with unknown causation of behavioral conditions.

Sudden cardiac dysfunction, anxiety, irritability, and the onset of depression are possible harmful long term side effects of stimulant drug therapy in children. The FDA Med Guide alert for stimulant and psychiatric medications in children mandates a change in direction. The new direction involves the Action Plan for Childhood Behavioral Conditions. This plan which is sponsored by the non-profit Coalition Against Overmedicating Our Youth (CAOOY) focuses on alternative bio- assessments and alternative treatment plans in children with behavioral conditions as well as prudent traditional medical approaches to determine the real cause of symptoms prior to premature drug therapy.

Many prominent psychiatrists and institutions across America recognize the significance of a new vision regarding the treatment of childhood behavioral symptoms. Universities in the United States are joining the prestigious Johns Hopkins University toward visionary change of psychiatric practice, involving comprehensive individualized psychiatric assessments, differential diagnosing as well as safe medication prescribing protocols in children.

Psychiatrists across America are now vehemently voicing their objection to the Diagnostic and Statistical Manual for Mental Disorders as a flawed guide for the practice of diagnosing Attention Deficit Disorders and psychiatric conditions. Currently, the Diagnostic and Statistical Manual does not recommend comprehensive alternative bio-assessments or differential diagnosing.

Dr. Thomas Insel, Director of the National Institute of Mental Health in Washington DC, made a bold statement on April 29, 2013..... referencing the assessment process in patients with mental disorders as " lacking validity". Under his direction, the Research Domain Criteria (RDoC), will become an added differential diagnosing criteria necessary to protect children from premature drug therapy.

Attention Deficit Disorder should be removed from the Diagnostic and Statistical Manual as a mental illness diagnosis. In doing so, state mental health systems will no longer be required to pay disability payments funded by Medicare taxpayer dollars to families with children diagnosed with Attention Deficit Disorder. Attention Deficit Disorder is a condition not a disease. This condition has a causation that requires a differential diagnosis through new comprehensive clinical bio-assessments.

Healthcare professionals within alternative as well as traditional medicine should unite and solve a child's behavioral condition prior to drug therapy. This union of clinical practitioners is essential for the implementation of the Action Plan for Childhood Behavioral Conditions, wherein the medical doctor or psychiatrist is the team leader of the child's treatment plan.

An independent physician, experienced in assessing childhood behavioral conditions, should conduct multiple bio-assessments to rule out nutritional, physiological and environmental risk factors. These assessments are outlined in the Action Plan for Childhood Behavioral Conditions. Results of these assessments should be forwarded to the team leader doctor. As a child's bio-assessments are being evaluated, a highly qualified therapist should perform critical emotional observations of the child and family unit. The therapist or psychotherapist should be knowledgeable in child behavior crisis management. Expert therapists in Focus Guided Imagery, Response Inhibition and Rational Emotive Behavior Therapy teaches a child techniques essential in strengthening the emotional thought process while reversing abnormal behavioral development. Mental health strength training classes should be implemented in all schools across America, just as physical strength training classes have been taught for decades.

Brain Wave Optimization or brain balancing is fast becoming a positive non-invasive neuro-feedback-type assessment, especially in the child population, and represents another new vision for the assessment of behavioral challenges. Brain Wave Optimization and Neurofeedback are noninvasive assessments aimed at altering brainwaves to normal rhythm or balance. Although Neurofeedback can be helpful, Brainwave Optimization may effectively train the brain to change itself and the initial session lasts approximately sixty minutes to map the area of the brain that is showing abnormal waves.

Brainwave Optimization technology, through the external placement of electrodes, collects energy from brainwaves. This energy is transferred into data that is converted into sound. During brain wave optimization, the brain's own sounds are played back to the brain, causing it to seek normal brainwave balance. This sound playback induces the brain back to a normal brainwave state.

Brainwave abnormalities may be the result of emotional or physical trauma. Through Brainwave Optimization, the technology can explain how and where trauma affects brain functionality. In doing so, the optimization process can target affected areas of the brain that need to be rebalanced. Brainwave Optimization technology represents another dimension for the new vision in assessing and treating behavioral symptoms. The brain observes itself through sound frequency computerization in order to return to normal cognitive functioning.

The new vision of assessing and ultimately treating children with behavioral challenges including ADHD, autism, depression and addictive behavior will give parents new hope for positive outcomes prior to premature drug therapy. Parents, educators, and all healthcare professionals should realize the benefit of comprehensive clinical assessments to find the cause of behavioral symptoms. Many cases of severe autism in the United States are being reversed due to the elimination of risk factors. Toxin overload in the digestive elimination systems of young children is one of the primary causes for the epidemic. Stress hormone accumulation in the body represents immediate evaluation. A whole foods diet free of Genetically Modified Organisms (GMO) artificial flavorings, colorings, and dyes must become the new food chain for young children in America.....foods that naturally help the body remove harmful free radical toxins, and help develop a focused healthy mind.

This new vision is supported by the non-profit Coalition Against Overmedicating Our Youth (CAOOY) and implemented through The Action Plan for Childhood Behavioral Conditions.

The action plan of compiling data from multiple bio-assessments as well as psychotherapy allows the team leader doctor to formulate the most effective treatment plan. In doing so, drug therapy in many cases may not be the primary course of treatment. As the implementation of the Action Plan for Childhood Behavioral Conditions proceeds, community by community, suicide rates will fall due to finding the cause of behavioral symptoms prior to premature drug therapy.

The current system of treating children with behavioral conditions requires immediate reform. No longer can Americans allow the deliberate mismanagement and exploitation of children with behavioral conditions. This new vision involving the new assessment and treatment of behavioral symptoms in children is attracting attention from many prestigious universities and physicians across the United States.

Children now have a voice to help find a cause for ADHD, autism, depression and addictive behavioral symptoms through this new vision of assessment and treatment.

- A new vision that no longer permits masking of their mental pain by drug therapy prior to a differential diagnosis involving multiple bio-assessments.
- A new vision that recommends a whole foods diet in young children
- A new vision that prohibits drug manufacturers from manipulating and enticing state mental health directors.
- A new vision that prohibits drug manufacturers from targeting and exploiting a child's mental health for profit.
- A new vision uniting American citizens to support appropriate medication prescribing protocols in the treatment of children with Attention Deficit Disorder and mental illness.

The Action Plan for Childhood Behavioral Conditions represents the template for this new vision of assessment and treatment, enabling the reformation of a system that is...

Over Medicating Our Youth

Notes

_____

_____

_____

_____

_____

_____

_____

_____

_____

_____

_____

_____

_____

_____

_____

_____

_____

_____

_____

_____

_____

Ask the Pharmacist • www.CAOOY.org

Glossary

1. Action plan – a sequence of steps that must be taken, or activities that must be performed well, for a strategy to succeed. An action plan has three major elements (1) specific tasks: what will be done and by whom (2) time horizon: when will it be done (3) resource allocation: what specific funds are available for specific activities.

2. Adverse Drug Reaction (ADR) – is an expression that describes harm associated with the use of given medications at a normal dosage during normal use. ADRs may occur following a single dose or prolonged administration of a drug or result from the combination of two or more drugs. The meaning of this expression differs from the meaning of "side effects", as this last expression might also imply that the effects can be beneficial. The study of ADRs is the concern of the field known as pharmacovigilance. An adverse drug event (ADE) refers to any injury caused by the drug (at normal dosage and/or due to overdose) and any harm associated with the use of drug (e.g. discontinuation of drug therapy)

3. Alternative medicine – is any healing practice that does not fall within the realm of traditional medical practice. Alternative medicine methods are diverse in their foundations and methodologies.

4. American Psychiatric Association (APA) – is a main professional organization of psychiatrists and trainee psychiatrists in the United States, and the most influential worldwide. The 38,000 members are mainly American but some are international. The association publishes various journals and pamphlets, as well as the Diagnostic and Statistical Manual of

Mental Disorders, or DSM. The DSM codifies psychiatric conditions and is used worldwide as a key guide for diagnosing disorders.

5. Amphetamine – is a scheduled CII Class synthetic stimulant used to treat attention-deficit hyperactivity disorder (ADHD). It may also be used for narcolepsy. Federal law prohibits giving this medicine to any person other than the person for whom it was prescribed.

6. Arsenic – a metallic element that forms a number of poisonous compounds, arsenic is found in nature at low levels mostly in compounds with oxygen, chlorine, and sulfur. These are called inorganic arsenic compounds. Most arsenic compounds have no smell or special taste.

7. Aspartame – is an artificial, non-saccharide sweetener used as a sugar substitute. Aspartame is a methyl ester of the aspartic acid phenylalanine dipeptide, and metabolizes in the body to formaldehyde and formic acid toxic compounds.

8. Attention Deficit Disorder (ADD) – is a condition, occurring mainly in children, characterized by hyperactivity, inability to concentrate, and impulsive or inappropriate behavior.

9. Brain Derived Neurotrophic Factor (BDNF) – is a secreted protein that, in humans, is encoded by the BDNF gene. BDNF is a member of the "neurotrophin" family of growth factors, which are related to the canonical "Nerve Growth Factor", NGF. Neurotrophic factors are found in the brain and the periphery.

10. Bipolar disorder – A mood disorder sometimes called manic – depressive illness or manic – depression that characteristically involves cycles of depression and elation or mania. Sometimes the mood switches from high to low and back again are dramatic and rapid, but more often they are gradual and slow, and intervals or normal mood may occur between the high (manic) and low (depressive) phases of the condition. The symptoms of both the depressive and manic cycles may be severe and often lead to impaired functioning.

11. Blood – brain – barrier system – is a separation of circulating blood from the brain extracellular fluid (BECF) in the central nervous system (CNS). It occurs along all capillaries and consists of tight junctions around the capillaries that do not exist in normal circulation. Endothelial cells restrict the diffusion of microscopic objects (e.g. bacteria) and large or hydrophilic molecules into the cerebrospinal fluid (CSF), while allowing the diffusion of small hydrophobic molecules (O2 CO2, hormones). Cells of the barrier actively transport metabolic products such as glucose across the barrier with specific proteins.

12. Carbon monoxide –is a colorless, odorless and tasteless gas which, in high concentrations, is toxic in humans. Carbon monoxide combines with oxygen to form carbon dioxide and ozone.

13. Centers of Disease Control and Prevention (CDC) – is a United States federal agency under the Department of Health and Human Services headquartered in Druid Hills, unincorporated DeKalb County, Georgia in Greater Atlanta. It works to protect public health and safety by providing information to enhance health decisions, and it promotes health through partnerships with state health departments and other organizations. The CDC focus national attention on developing and applying disease prevention and control (especially infectious disease and food borne pathogens and other microbial infections), environmental health, occupational safety and health, health promotion, injury prevention and education activities designed to improve the health of the people of the United States. The CDC is the United States' national public health institute and is a founding member of the International Association of National Public Health Institutes IANPHI.

14. Centers for Medicaid and Medicare Services (CMS) – previously known as the Health Care Financing Administration (HCFA), is a federal agency within the United States Department of Health and Human Services (DHHS) that administers the Medicare program and works in partnership with state governments to administer Medicaid, the State Children's Health Insurance Program (SCHIP), and health insurance portability standards. In addition to these programs, CMS has other responsibilities, including the administrative simplification standards from the Health Portability and Accountability Act of 1996 (HIPPA), quality standards in long-term care facilities through its survey and certification process, and clinical laboratory quality standards under the Clinical Laboratory Improvements Amendments.

15. Coalition Against Overmedicating Our Youth (CAOOY) - is a nonprofit educational health and wellbeing organization whose mission is to help parents help their children determine cause of behavioral challenges by ruling out nutritional, physiological and environmental risk factors prior to premature drug therapy. Additionally, CAOOY provides free medication consultations as well as bio-assessment recommendations.

16. Cognitive Behavioral Therapy – is an action oriented form of psychosocial therapy that assumes that maladaptive, or faulty, thinking patterns cause maladaptive behavior and "negative" emotions. (Maladaptive behavior is behavior that is counter- productive or interferes with everyday living.) The treatment focuses on changing on individual's thoughts (cognitive patterns) in order to change his or her behavior and emotional state.

17. Dermatophytosis (ringworm) – is a clinical condition caused by fungal infection of the skin in humans, pets such as cats, and domesticated animals such as sheep and cattle. The term "ringworm" is a misnomer, since the condition is caused by fungi of several different species and not by parasitic worms. The fungi that cause parasitic infection (dermatophytes) feed on keratin, the material found in the outer layer of skin, hair, and nails. The fungi thrive on skin that is warm and moist, but may also survive directly on the outside of hair shafts or in their interiors. In pets, the fungus responsible for the disease survives in skin and on the outer surface of hairs. It has been estimated that currently up to twenty percent of the population may be infected by ringworm or one of the other dermatophytoses.

18. Diagnostic and Statistical Manual of Mental Disorders (DSM) – Many mental health professionals use the manual to determine and help communicate a patient's diagnosis after an evaluation; hospitals, clinics, and insurance companies in the United States generally require a 'five axis' DSM diagnosis of all the patients treated. The DSM can be used clinically in this way, and also to categorize patients using diagnostic criteria for research purposes.

19. Differential diagnosis – is a systematic diagnostic method used to identify the presence of an entity where multiple alternatives are possible (and the process may be termed differential diagnostic procedure), and may also refer to any of the included candidate alternatives (which may also be termed candidate condition). This method is essentially a process of elimination, or at least, rendering of the probabilities of candidate conditions to negligible levels. In this sense, probabilities are, in fact, imaginative parameters in the mind or hardware of the diagnostician or system, while in reality the target (such as a patient) either has a condition or not with an actual probability of either 0 or 100%. Differential diagnostic procedures are used by physicians, psychiatrists, and other trained medical professionals to diagnose the specific disease in a patient, or, at least, to eliminate any imminently life-threatening conditions. Differential diagnosis can be regarded as implementing aspects of the hypothetico-deductive method in the sense that the potential presence of candidate diseases or conditions can be viewed as hypotheses which are further processes as being true or false.

20. Diffusion Tensor Imaging (DTI) – a refinement of magnetic resonance imaging that allows the doctor to measure the flow of water and track the pathways of white matter in the brain. DTI is able to detect abnormalities in the brain that do not show up on standard MRI scans.

21. Drug Enforcement Administration (DEA) – is a federal law enforcement agency under the United States Department of Justice, tasked with combating drug smuggling and use within the United States. Not only is the DEA the lead agency for domestic enforcement of the Controlled Substances Act, sharing concurrent jurisdiction with the Federal Bureau of Investigation (FBI) and Immigration Customs Enforcement (ICE), it also has sole responsibility for coordinating and pursuing U.S. drug investigations abroad.

22. Dysthymia (Minor depression) – also known as neurotic depression, is a mood disorder consisting of chronic depression, with less severe but longer lasting symptoms than major depressive disorder. It is a serious state of chronic depression, which persists for at least two years; it is less acute and severe major depressive disorder. As dysthymia is a chronic disorder, sufferers may experience symptoms for many years before it is diagnosed, if diagnosis occurs at all. As a result, they may believe that depression is part of their character, so they may not even discuss their symptoms with doctors, family members, or friends.

23. Eicosapentaenoic acid (EPA or also icosapentaenoic acid) – is an omega – 3 fatty acid. In physiological literature, it is given the name 20:5(n-3). It is also has the trivial name timnodonic acid. In chemical structure, EPA is a carboxylic acid.

20. Carbon chain and five cis double bonds- the first double bond is located at the third carbon from the omega end. EPA and its metabolites act in the body largely by their interactions with the metabolites or arachidonic acid. It is obtained in the human diet by eating oily fish or fish oil – e.g., cod liver, herring, mackerel, salmon, menhaden, and sardine. It is also found in human breast milk.

24. Emotion – an affective state of consciousness in which joy, sorrow, fear, hate, or the like, is experienced, as distinguished from cognitive and volitional states of consciousness.

25. Emotional pain – is a particular kind of psychological pain, more closely related to emotions. In the fields of social psychology and personality psychology, the term social pain is used to denote emotional pain caused by harm or threat to social connection; bereavement, embarrassment, shame, and hurt feelings are subtypes of social pain.

26. Etiology – is the study of causation or origination. The word is derived from the Greek "giving a reason for".

27. FD&C dye – is an azo-dye that may be associated with increased allergy sensitization and hyperactive behavior.

28. Food and Drug Administration (FDA) – is an agency of the United States Department of Health and Human Services, one of the United States federal executive departments. The FDA is responsible for protecting and promoting public health through the regulation and supervision of food safety, tobacco products, dietary supplements, prescription and over-the- counter pharmaceutical drugs (medications), vaccines, biopharmaceuticals, blood transfusions, medical devices, electromagnetic radiation emitting devices (ERED), veterinary products, and cosmetics.

29. Formaldehyde – is an aqueous solution with carcinogenic properties and a byproduct of aspartame metabolism in the human body.

30. Formic acid – is a carboxylic acid naturally occurring in bee and ant venom. Formic acid is a byproduct of aspartame metabolism and may cause optic nerve as well as kidney damage as a result of methanol poisoning.

31. Glutathione (GSH) – is a tripeptide that contains an unusual peptide linkage between the amine group of cysteine (which is attached by normal peptide linkage to a glycine) and the carboxyl group of the glutamate side-chain. It is an antioxidant, preventing damage to important cellular components caused by reactive oxygen species such as free radicals and peroxides.

32. Government Accountability Office (GAO) – is the audit, evaluation, and investigation arm of the United States Congress. It is part of the legislative branch of the United States government.

33. Guided Imagery – an alternative medicine technique in which patients use their imagination to visualize improved health or to "attach" a disease, such as a tumor, some studies indicated that the positive thinking can have an effect on disease outcome, so this technique is now utilized as "complimentary medicine" in some oncology centers and other medical facilities.

34. Homeostasis – is the property of a system that regulates its internal environment and tends to maintain a stable, constant condition of properties like temperature or pH. It can be either an open or a closed system.

35. Homotoxicology – is an approach to healing that integrates the treatment principles of homeopathy with the diagnostic approach of allopathic medicine. Developed over fifty years ago in Germany, homotoxicology is becoming more widely practiced in the United States. Practitioners trained in homotoxicology offer homeopathic remedies for a variety of health concerns. The goal of treatment in homotoxicology is to detoxify the body and restore the body's natural biorhythms. For those with health challenges, homotoxicology maintains that health cannot be achieved without ridding the body of toxins. Homotoxicology involves using homeopathic remedies to facilitate the removal of toxins and stimulate the body's capacity to heal itself.

36. Informed consent – is a phrase often used in law to indicate that the consent a person gives meets certain minimum standards. As a literal matter, in the absence of fraud, it is redundant. An informed consent can be said to have been given based upon a clear appreciation and understanding of the facts, implications, and future consequences of an action. In order to give informed consent, the individual concerned must have adequate reasoning faculties and be in possession of all relevant facts at the time consent is given. Impairments to reasoning and judgment which may make it impossible for someone to give informed consent include such factors as basic intellectual or emotional immaturity, high levels of stress such as PTSD or as severe mental retardation, severe mental illness, intoxication, severe sleep deprivation, Alzheimer's disease, or being in a coma.

37. Irritable bowel syndrome (IBS) – is a common disorder that affects the large intestine (colon). Irritable bowel syndrome commonly causes cramping, abdominal pain, bloating, gas, diarrhea, and constipation. Despite these uncomfortable signs and symptoms, IBS does not cause permanent damage to the colon. Most people with IBS find that symptoms improve as they learn to control their condition. Only a small number of people with irritable bowel syndrome have disabling and signs and symptoms.

38. Malabsorption – the impaired absorption of nutrients into the blood stream from the small intestine. Malabsorption can be specific and involve sugars, fats, proteins, or vitamins. Alternatively, malabsorption can be general and nonspecific.

39. Medical Marijuana Card – is a state issued identification card that enables a patient with a doctor's recommendation to obtain, possess, or cultivate cannabis for medicinal use. These cards are issued by a state or county in which medical marijuana is considered legal. Typically, a patient is required to pay a fee to the state in order to obtain a medical marijuana card. In most states that allow medical cannabis, the maximum length that a medical marijuana card is considered legal is 12 months. The patient must renew their ID card.

40. Neurotransmitters – are endogenous chemicals that transmit signals from a neuron to a target cell across a synapse. Neurotransmitters are packaged into synaptic vesicles clustered beneath the membrane on the presynaptic side of synapse, and are released into the synaptic cleft, where they bind to receptors in the membrane on the postsynaptic side of the synapse. Release of neurotransmitters usually follows arrival of an action potential at the synapse, but may also follow graded electrical potentials. Low level "baseline" release also occurs without electrical stimulation. Neurotransmitters are synthesized from plentiful and simple precursors, such as amino acids, which are readily available from the diet and which require only a small number of biosynthetic steps to convert.

41. Parasitic worms – often referred to as helminthes are a division of eukaryotic parasites. They are worm-like organisms that live and feed of living hosts, receiving nourishment and protection while disrupting their hosts' nutrient absorption, causing weakness and disease. Those that live inside the digestive tract are called intestinal parasites. They can live inside humans as well as other animals.

42. Pathophysiology – is the study of the changes of normal mechanical, physiological, and biochemical functions, either caused by a disease, or resulting from an abnormal syndrome. More formally, it is the branch of medicine which deals with any disturbance of body functions, caused by disease or prodromal syndrome.

43. Prefrontal cortex –is the anterior part of the frontal lobes of the brain responsible for cognitive behavioral function.

44. Probiotics – are live microorganisms thought to beneficial to the host organism. According to the currently adopted definition by FAO/WHO, probiotics are: "Live microorganisms which when administered in adequate amounts confer a health benefit on the host". Lactic acid bacteria (LAB) and bifidobacteria are the most common types of microbes used as probiotics; but certain yeasts and bacilli may also be used. Probiotics are commonly consumed as part of fermented foods with specially added active live cultures: such as in yogurt, soy yogurt, or as dietary supplements. At the start of the 20th century, probiotics were thought to beneficially affect the host by improving its intestinal microbial balance, thus inhibiting pathogens and toxin producing bacteria. Today, specific health effects are being investigated and documented including alleviation of chronic intestinal inflammatory diseases, prevention, and treatment of pathogen-induced diarrhea, urogenital infections, and atopic diseases.

45. Prodromal syndrome – a prodrome is an early symptom that might indicate the start of a disease before specific symptoms occur.

46. Psychoneuroendocrinology – is the clinical study of hormone fluctuations and their relationship to human behavior. It may be viewed from the perspective of psychiatry, where in certain mood disorders, there are associated neuroendocrine or hormonal changes affecting the brain. It may also be viewed from the perspective of endocrinology, where certain endocrine disorders can be associated with psychiatric illness. Brain dysfunctions such as in the hypothalamus can affect the endocrine system, which in turn can result in psychiatric symptoms. This complex blend of psychiatry neurology and endocrinology is needed to comprehensively understand and treat psychiatric illnesses of non-psychological etiology.

47. Psyllium seed husks – also known as psyllium are portions of the seeds of the plant Plantago ovate a native of India. They are hydroscopic (that is they absorb water expanding and become mucilaginous. Ayurveda recommends its use for colon cleansing/bowel regulation as well as for better blood circulation. Psyllium seed husks are indigestible and are a source of soluble dietary fiber. They are used to relieve constipation, irritable bowel syndrome, and diarrhea. They are also used as a regular dietary supplement to improve and maintain regular GI transit. The inert bulk of the husks help provide a constant volume of solid material irrespective of other aspects of the diet or any disease condition of the gut. Some recent research is also showing them to be promising in lowering cholesterol and controlling diabetes.

48. Radon gas – is a chemical element with the atomic number 86, and is represented by the symbol Rn. It is a radioactive, colorless, odorless, tasteless, noble gas occurring naturally as the decay product of uranium or thorium.

49. Rapid eye movement (R.E.M. sleep) – is a normal stage of sleep characterized by the rapid and random movement of the eyes. REM sleep is classified into two categories: tonic and phasic. It was identified and defined by Nathaniel Kleitman, Eugene Aserinsky, and Jon Birtwell in the early 1950's. Criteria for REM sleep include rapid eye movement, but also low muscle tone and a rapid, low-voltage EEF; these features are easily discernible in a polysomnogram, the sleep study typically done for patients with suspected sleep disorders.

50. Rational emotive behavior therapy (REBT) – is a comprehensive, active-directive, philosophically and empirically based psychotherapy which focuses on resolving emotional and behavioral problems and disturbances and enabling people to lead happier and more fulfilling lives. REBT was created and developed by the American psychotherapist and psychologist Albert Ellis who was inspired by many of the teachings of Asian, Greek, Roman, and modern philosophers. REBT is one form of cognitive behavior therapy (CBT) and was first expounded by Ellis in the mid-1950; development continued until his death in 2007.

51. Self esteem – is a term in psychology to reflect a person's overall evaluation or appraisal of his or her own worth. Self – esteem encompasses beliefs and emotions such as triumph, despair, pride, and shame.

52. Stimulant drug – also referred to as psychostimulants are psychoactive drugs which induce temporary improvements in either mental or physical function or both. Examples of these kinds of effects may include enhanced alertness, wakefulness, and locomotion, among others. Due to their effects typically having an "up" quality to them, stimulants are also occasionally referred to as "uppers". Depressants or "downers", which decrease mental and/or physical function, are in stark contrast to stimulants and are considered to be their functional opposites. Stimulants are widely used throughout the world as prescription medicines and as illicit substances for recreational use or abuse.

53. Swimmer's itch – also known as Lake Itch, duck itch, cercarial dermatitis, and Schistosome cercarial dermatitis, is a short-term, immune reaction occurring in the skin of humans that have been infected by water-borne schistosomatidae. Symptoms, which include itchy, raised papules, commonly occur within hours of infection and do not generally last more than a week. A number of different flatworm parasites in the family Schistosomatidae are what cause swimmer's itch. These parasites use both freshwater snails and vertebrates as hosts in their parasitic life cycles. Since, it was first described in Michigan in 1928, swimmer's itch has been reported from around the world.

54. Texas Medication Algorithm Project (TMAP) – is a decision tree medical algorithm, the design of which was based on the expert opinions of mental health specialists. It has provided and rolled out a set of psychiatric management guidelines for doctors treating certain mental disorders within Texas' publicly-funded mental health care system, along with manuals relating to each of them. The algorithms commence after diagnosis and cover pharmacological treatment.

55. Toxoplasma gondii – is a species of parasitic protozoa in the genus Toxoplasma. The definitive host of T.gondii is the cat, but the parasite can be carried by many warm-blooded animals (bird or mammals, including humans). Toxoplasmosis, the disease of which T. gondii is the causative agent, is usually minor and self-limiting but can have serious or even fatal effects on a fetus whose mother first contracts with the disease during pregnancy or on an immunocompromised human or cat.

56. Tyrosine hydroxylase – is the enzyme responsible for catalyzing the conversion of the amino acid L-tyrosine to dihydroxyphenylalanine (DOPA). It does so using tetrahydrobioperin as a coenzyme. DOPA is a precursor for dopamine, which, in turn, is a precursor for norepinephrine (noradrenaline) and epinephrine (adrenaline). In humans, tyrosine hydroxylase is encoded by the TH gene.

57. United States Department of Health and Human Services (HHS) – is a Cabinet department of United States government with the goal of protecting the health of all Americans and providing essential human services. Its mission is "Improving the health, safety, and well-being of America." Before the separate federal Department of Education was created in 1979, it was called the Department of Health, Education, and Welfare (HEW).

58. Whole foods – are foods that are unprocessed and unrefined, or processed and refined as little as possible, before being consumed. Whole foods typically do not contain added ingredients, such as salt, carbohydrates, or fat. Examples of whole foods include unpolished grains, beans, fruits, vegetables, and non-homogenized dairy products. Although originally all human food was whole food, one of the earliest uses of the term post-industrial age was in 1960 when the leading organic good organization called the Soil Association opened a shop in the name selling organic and whole grain products in London, UK. The term is often confused with organic food, but whole foods are not necessarily organic, nor are organic foods necessarily whole. The United States Food and Drug Administration defines whole grains as cereal grains containing the bran, endosperm, and germ of the original grain. Federal Dietary Guidelines issued by the Center for Nutrition Policy and Promotion in 2005 recommended the consumption of at least three servings of whole grains each day, as there is evidence that they help cut risk of cancer and heart disease.

59. World Health Organization (WHO) – is a specialized agency of the United Nations (UN) that is concerned with international public health. It was established on 7 April 1948, with headquarters in Geneva, Switzerland and is a member of the United Nations Development Group. Its predecessor, the Health Organization, was an agency of the League of Nations.

References

CHAPTER 1

1. http://www.ncbI.nlm.nih.gov/PUBMED/7771916
2. Focus on the Family, p141

CHAPTER 2

3. http://Clinical-excellence/ Johns Hopkins University School of Medicine, Department of Psychiatry and Behavioral Sciences
4. www.scientificamerican.com
5. http://psychcentral.com/lib
6. www.scientificamerican.com
7. http://www.psychsearch.net/teenscreen.html
8. http://www.psychsearch.net/teenscreen.html
9. http://www.cchr.org/cchr-reports/harming-youth
10. http://en.wikipedia.org/w/index.php?title=New_Freedom_Commission
11. http://www.cchrint.org/tag/allen-jones/
12. http://www.cchrint.org/tag/allen-jones
13. http://www.cchrint.org/tag/allen-jones
14. http://www.cchrint.org/tag/allen-jones
15. http://www.cchrint.org/tag/allen-jones
16. http://www.psychsearch.net/psych_news/
17. http://www.gao.gov/products/GAO-12-270T

CHAPTER 3

18. http://www.cchrint.org/tag/stimulants/
19. http://www.cchrint.org/tag/stimulants/
20. http://www.healthguideinfo.com/causes-of-add-adhd/
21. http://whychiropractic
22. www.epa.gov/radiation/radionuclides/radon.html
22a www.hopkinschildrens.org/ADHD-Symptoms-Persist-for-Most-Young-Children-Despite-Treatment.aspx
23. http://learnweb.harvard.edu/alps/thinking/docs/article1.html

CHAPTER 4

24. http://www.ritalindeath.com/
25. http://www.ritalindeath.com

CHAPTER 5

26. http://www.psychsearch.net/psych_news/?p=2035
27. http://www.psychsearch.net/psych_news/?p=2035
28. http://www.psychsearch.net/psych_news/?p=2035
29. 2http://www.psychsearch.net/psych_news/?p=2035

CHAPTER 7

30. http://www.bbb.org/charity-reviews/national/human-services

CHAPTER 8

31. www.AJCN.org/content
32. http://discovery.mnhs.org
33. Puri, Basant K. (2006) High-resolution M.R.I. In the study of fatty acid interventions in schizophrenia, depression, chronic fatigue syndrome and Huntington's Disease. Int. Rev. Psychiatry
34. Lafourcade, M. et al. Nutritional omega-3 deficiency abolishes endocannabinoid-neural functions. Nature Neuroscience(2011) 14:345
35. www.glutathionediseasecure.com/
36. http://www.holistic-wellness-basics.com/parasite

37. Levinger, B. "Nutrition, Health & Learning: Current Issues and Trends."
38. World Health Organization, Technical Series Report 749 "Prevention and Control of Intestinal Parasitic Infections"
39. http://en.wikipedia.org/wiki/Brain-derived_neurotrophic_factor

CHAPTER 9
40. www.colleenmurphy.massagetherapy.com/spectravision
41. http://www.barrygreenphd.com/
42. http://www.webmd.com/depression/guide/depression-children
43. http://www.depression-guide.com/rational-emotive-behavior-therapy.htm

CHAPTER 10
44. www.savethechildren.org